Women of the Bible
Volume 3

Helpless & Hurting

by

Shirley M. Starr

Copyright © 2004

Shirley M. Starr

Starr Publications

ISBN   0-9728162-3-2

First Printing   April, 2004

NOTE: All Bible references taken from
the Authorized Version (KJV).

Printed in the U.S.A. by
Morris Publishing
3212 East Highway 30
Kearney, NE 68847
1-800-650-7888

Dedication

This book is dedicated
to

all of the helpless and hurting women we have
counseled who have experienced tragedy,
incest, rape, sorrow, widowhood,
single-parenting, loneliness, etc.
The courage and faith in God with which you have
followed the Bible and faced your circumstances
have been an inspiration to me.
I salute you with this volume!

Preface

Many Bible women wore the garments of heartache, sorrow, grief, and tragedy in their personal lives. Like ladies of today, some faced barrenness, the loss of a child, or an early widowhood. Others wore the scars of abuse, rape, or incest. God knows the evil heart of sinful man, so He left these ladies' biographies in His Holy Word as examples to us.

They learned, like the Psalmist David, to say, "In the day when I **cried** thou answeredst me, and strengthenedst me with strength **in my soul**." *(Psa. 138 :3)* Many affirmed that "weeping may endure for a night, but joy cometh in the morning." *(Psa. 30:5)*

Though helpless and hurting, they experienced the consolation of God's protection, His provision, and His promise to never leave or forsake them. These ladies are memorable because they rose above their miserable circumstances.

> 'When life is difficult, it's easy to give up; but giving up is the worst thing we can do. A professor of history said, "If Columbus had turned back, nobody would have blamed him -- but nobody would have remembered him either." If you want to be memorable, sometimes you have to be miserable.'
> *(Wiersbe, p. 30)*

May these **helpless and hurting** women encourage you, dear lady, to keep your focus on Jesus Christ throughout your time of misery and suffering. "Though I walk in the midst of trouble, thou wilt revive me. . ." *(Psa. 138:7a)*

Table of Contents
Women of the Bible, Volume 3
Helpless & Hurting

Title page
Copyright page
Dedication page
Preface

	Page
1. Hagar	1
2. Dinah	10
3. Jephthah's Daughter	18
4. Naomi	27
5. Hannah	38
6. Rizpah	47
7. Tamar	53
8. The Widow of Zarephath	60
9. The Shunamite Woman	67
10. The Syrophenician Woman	77

Sources
How to Order additional copies

Chapter 1

HAGAR

The Single Parent
"A Desperate Woman Who
Exchanged a Bottle for a Well."

Facts

Husband:	Abraham
Children:	Ishmael
Occupation:	Handmaid, servant, slave, concubine
Her name means:	"Fugitive" or "immigrant"

Background   (Gen. 16:1)

In our study of Sarah in volume 1, we recall that Sarah had a handmaid named Hagar. Hagar was a personal maid, or female servant, and a native of Egypt. Legend says that she was the daughter of Pharaoh, king of Egypt. Had Sarah won her to the Lord while in Egypt, or was she a gift from Pharaoh?

Hagar's name means "fugitive," "immigrant," or "flight." We will see how accurately she lives up to that name. She was to become a thorn in Sarah's side. Little did she know what being Sarah's handmaid would entail!

Sarah's Folly   (Gen. 16:2-6; Prov. 30:21-23)

As Sarah ran ahead of God, ignoring the directive will of God, she followed the laws and customs of the old land. After living in Canaan for ten years and bearing no children, she planned to give Hagar as a concubine or "secondary wife" to

Abraham so they could finally have children. But what about God's promise to them? We do not see either Sarah or Hagar seeking God's guidance. Sarah sought a human solution to her problem.

Isn't that just like us today? Often we fail to seek God's guidance or godly counseling about a decision or situation in our lives. We act impulsively instead of waiting upon the Lord. We go for counsel to people who say what we want to hear instead of accepting what God's Word says. Sarah's decision, like those we make, greatly affected the entire family, causing much grief and turmoil.

We do not see Hagar challenging or questioning the plan. Perhaps she thought, "What do I have to lose? We are out in the middle of nowhere and there are no other men to notice me here!" Undoubtedly, she recognized that Abraham was a kind and caring man, and she admired and respected him. Did she even have the right to challenge Sarah?

After Hagar conceived, she gloated, despising her mistress, Sarah. She may have thought, "I did something even Sarah couldn't do." Pride set in causing great turmoil in the home. Sarah had created a rivalry between her and Hagar with Hagar suffering far more. Strife and jealousy abounded between the two. Proverbs 30:21-23 describes the situation well, saying the earth is "disquieted... for a servant when he reigneth; ...and an handmaid that is heir to her mistress." These women could not stand the sight of each other anymore. Imagine every day Sarah having to face her own sorrow of barrenness and Hagar's joy of conception. Now what could she do? She was unable to bear the trial any longer! Her impulsiveness and impatience had caused her real trouble!

She ran to Abraham and explained the situation, blaming him. Abraham told her to do whatever pleased her. Can't you just see him throwing up his hands and thinking, "Nothing can make this woman happy!" He washed his hands of the entire situation, instructing Sarah to handle it.

Hagar's First Flight <small>(Gen. 16:6-14)</small>

Sarah approached Hagar and dealt "hardly" with her. It was a pretty harsh and angry scene between the two women, so harsh in fact, that Hagar fled without permission. Had she rebelled? Remember Hagar was still under Sarah's authority as a handmaid even though she was the victim of Sarah's conniving scheme. Life just did not seem fair!

Scripture tells us she fled into the wilderness on the way to Shur. What was a pregnant, single woman going to do? Where was she going to go? She had no job, no one to care for her, and no place to live. But God cared! He provided a "fountain of water in the wilderness" and sent an angel of the Lord to deal with her and give her direct-guidance. Genesis 16:8 shows us He knew her name and vocation "Hagar, Sarai's maid." We need never fear that God is unaware of what we are facing or where we are at a certain stage of life. He deeply cares and understands. Maybe Hagar was a "nobody" to man, just a servant, a handmaid. But, she was "somebody" to God. He knew all about her trial!

The angel asked her where she had come from and where she was going. Hagar truthfully told the angel that she was fleeing from her mistress. The angel proceeded to give her explicit directions, perhaps directions she really did not want to hear. He told her, "Return to thy mistress, and **submit** thyself under her hands." She was to get back under her authority. This would be extremely hard for her, given their caustic conflict. However, the Lord knew she could do it, and He would give her the strength **to do** it.

Many times our authorities (husbands, employers, pastors, etc.) make decisions we do not understand or want to follow. We, like Hagar, tend to rebel and want to run from our situations. However, God has a purpose for the authorities in our lives and knows we will grow by obedience to them, even through difficult situations. Hebrews 13:17a says, "Obey them that have the rule over you, and submit yourselves: for they watch for your souls."

Though the angel gave Hagar hard counsel and direction, he also promised to multiply her seed so that it could not be numbered. Wow! This was the same promise God had made to Abraham! The Lord even told her what she was to name the child – "Ishmael." Ishmael means "God shall hear." God took notice of **her** situation, **her** affliction, and **her** trial. He understood and He cared for her as an individual.

God takes notice of our trials and afflictions also. Their purpose is to promote our growth and increase our ability to help others. Second Corinthians 1:4 promises us that because of our tribulations, we will be able to comfort others "by the comfort wherewith we ourselves are comforted of God." We can depend on Him to give comfort, direction, and guidance during the stormy seasons of our lives.

Realizing God was in this, Hagar said, "Thou God seest me…" The name of the well was even called Beerlahairoi or the "well of Him that liveth and seeth me." What an omniscient, omnipresent, omnipotent God we have! He knows, He is present, and He has the power to help in any and all situations! Hagar obeyed the Lord and returned. Imagine the difficulty of returning! She had to put down her pride and submit once again to her mistress! May God help us to swallow our pride and submit to the authorities in our own lives.

Hagar's Return   (Gen. 16:15-16; 21:5, 9-12; Gal. 4:29-30)

Hagar returned and submitted herself unto Sarah. Scripture remains silent concerning their ongoing relationship. Hagar bore Ishmael when Abraham was 86 years old. Eleven years had passed since he and Sarah had left Haran. Imagine Abraham's excitement over the birth of Ishmael! Although this son was not the seed God had promised, it was still his blood and carried his name. Perhaps Sarah came to love and nourish this child, even claiming him as her own just as Rachel later did after her handmaid bore Dan. *(Gen. 30:3-6)* Perhaps the child healed the old wounds between the women...until...

Fourteen years later Sarah bore Isaac. When rejoicing should have been the order of the day, once again jealousy returned and reared its ugly head. Sarah saw Ishmael mocking Isaac! Had he picked up an attitude from his mother? Well, Sarah was not about to put up with it!

This frustrating home situation created reactions from Sarah, Abraham, and God. Sarah became very angry and told Abraham to cast out Hagar and Ishmael. Abraham was grief-stricken, because after all, Ishmael was his son, too. God told Abraham to fulfill Sarah's request, because his seed was to be "called in Isaac." The sowing and reaping continued for Abraham, as he would never see Ishmael again. Hagar and Ishmael had abused their privileges by mocking Isaac and now were forced to forfeit them by leaving the only home they had ever known.

Hagar's Final Departure (Gen. 21:14-21; Jn. 4:14; Gal. 4:22-25)

What a sad situation! Abraham rose early in the morning and gave Hagar food and a bottle of water. Perhaps he had spent a restless night, knowing what God had instructed him to do and how hard it would be to obey. Hagar now became a single parent and Ishmael a fatherless child. She was now in the "wilderness experience" of her life and "wandered in the wilderness of Beersheba." *(Gen. 21:14)* She no longer had a position as Sarah's maid, no rights to Abraham's name, no one to provide for her and the child. Such was Hagar's plight!

> 'If she have given a maid to her husband and she has borne children and afterwards that maid has made herself equal with her mistress, because she has borne children her mistress shall not sell her for money, she shall reduce her to bondage and count her among the female slaves.'
> *(Laws of King Hammurabi, Karssen, p. 19)*

Running out of water, she cast the child under a shrub. Great sorrow, anguish, and loneliness overtook her and she wept. She did not want to **see** the death of her own child. But just when her situation became desperate, God came on the scene again. He asked, "What's wrong, Hagar?" Notice He called her by name again. Her extremity had now become God's opportunity. Sometimes it takes a "wilderness experience" to get our attention. But God knows our name and where we are. Our extremity becomes His opportunity.

God knew all about it. (Scripture says He had heard the voice of the lad.) God was interested in her personally, and God had power to help. Encouraging her with a word of assurance, "Fear not," He gave her a positive command and told her to "lift up the lad." Though Ishmael had no human father, he had a heavenly Father. His heavenly Father promised to make a great nation of him.

Perhaps your earthly father has passed on, or maybe you have a broken relationship with your father. Don't be dismayed! You have a heavenly Father Who loves you and cares for you. He wants to fellowship with you and to meet your every need. He waits for you to acknowledge Him daily and spend time with Him. Renew your strength through Him, and give Him time to heal the sorrow or broken relationship in your life. All things are possible with the heavenly Father!

God wants us to know that He is with us in our "wilderness experiences" and does not want us to wallow in self-pity and become useless to Him. Notice He gave specific directions to Hagar and she obeyed.

It was only after she obeyed that she saw the well of water. God honored her obedience. She had been so taken up with herself and her trial that she had never seen the well! The well had been there all the time. "And God opened her eyes…" *(Gen. 21:19)* She then gave the lad a drink.

We need to keep our focus on God during our trials and afflictions so we will see the "well of water" He has prepared for us. Then, like Hagar, we will be able to share that water with others.

Years later, Hagar took Ishmael a wife from the land of Egypt, perhaps displaying a heart for her heathen land instead of a heart totally committed to the Lord. What a mistake! Did God allow her to be cast out to keep Abraham's house pure and separated? Or had she just returned to her own homeland and taken up the old customs again?

Nothing more is heard from Hagar's life after this, though her life is verified in the New Testament when Paul used her to show the difference between law and grace in Galatians 4. The Arab nations were founded by Ishmael, whereas, the Israelites were descendants from Isaac – and Ishmael still despises Isaac.

Did she ever find true happiness? Did she use her "wilderness experience" to encourage and to witness to others? Did she learn to rely and depend upon God? Her greatest joy had to be in knowing that there was a loving God Who cared and provided for her.

Conclusions

There are many lessons from helpless and hurting Hagar. We know a new position tempted her. We need to beware of enticement in our own lives. First Corinthians 10:12 says, "Wherefore let him that thinketh he standeth take heed lest he fall." James 1:14 cautions, "But every man is tempted when he is drawn away of his own lust, and enticed." Hagar had many good things going for her in the beginning, but let pride overtake her spirit.

God is sovereign and has divine control in everyone's life. His will is sometimes worked out by harsh methods. It sometimes takes a "wilderness experience" to get our attention.

During the "wilderness experiences" in our lives, God is there, and He knows we are there. He gives strength, comfort, encouragement, and direction, even through the hardest days and hours. He does not forsake us when we get out of His will. He is there just like He was for Hagar, wooing us back to Himself and pointing us to Scriptural submission. How about you? Are you suffering through a "wilderness experience" right now in your own life? What did Jesus do during His "wilderness experience?" According to Matthew 4, He kept His focus on the Lord and the Word of God. What a challenge to us as believers! Do we even know enough of the Word to help us through our time of trial? Have we memorized and hidden the precious truths in our hearts?

Often we become preoccupied with ourselves during a time of trial and fail to witness or serve. It is through these times that our families, friends, and the world are watching us to see our reaction during testing. What an opportunity we have to reflect Christ, showing our dependence on Him. We must take our eyes off the trial we face and get our eyes back on Him. Hebrews 12:2 says that we should be "looking unto Jesus the author and finisher of our faith." Hagar only saw the well when she took her eyes off her trial. She missed the Lord. We dare not miss seeing Him in the midst of **our** trial.

God is our Provider. He gave Hagar a well **twice**. Our extremity often becomes His great opportunity to manifest Himself to us in mighty and wonderful ways! Dear sister, allow the Lord to provide for you during your trial! According to Hebrews 2:18, because Jesus Himself faced temptation, He is able to help you through it! "For in that he himself hath suffered being tempted, he is able to succour them that are tempted." The word "succour" means to "run to help, relieve, aid, embrace." He ran to Hagar's problem!

What else does our God provide during our trial? He promises not to put more on us than we can bear, **and**, He promises a way of escape! "...but God is faithful, who will not suffer you to be tempted above that ye are able; but will with the temptation also make a way to escape, that ye may be able to bear it!" *(1 Cor. 10:13b)*

Lastly, God cares for us as individuals. He knew Hagar's name and position. He knows our name and position. He knew Hagar was a single parent and faced lonely times and a lack of security. Dear lady, if you are a single parent, remember that God will be a father to your children and give you direct guidance. Psalm 10:14 says, "...thou art the helper of the fatherless." Likewise, Psalm 68:4-5 tells us to sing and rejoice unto God, and calls Him, "A father of the fatherless, and a judge of the widows, is God in his holy habitation." Scripture promises us "he relieveth the fatherless and widow." *(Psa.146:9)* What comfort the Word of God affords!

Be encouraged to keep your children in church where they will see other godly Christian men and be under their influence. You need the local church as a haven and a comfort station in your life. Teach your children to run to God at any time, to depend upon Him for answers to their problems, and instruct them in what the Bible says about the fatherless. Maintain a close personal walk with the Lord yourself. Point out all the answered prayers to your children, and keep a positive spirit, not harboring a bitter spirit, or a "poor me" attitude. Let them see the joy of Jesus that comes from serving others! Let your extremity become **His opportunity!** Look for Jesus in your trial.

Hagar's Roles

1. Handmaiden
2. Slave
3. Surrogate mother
4. Concubine
5. Immigrant

Hagar's Character Traits

1. Honesty
2. Obedience
3. Pride
4. Jealousy
5. Rebellion

Chapter 2

DINAH

The Curious Teenager
"The Woman Whose Sightseeing
Had Fatal Results"

Facts
Husband:	None
Children:	None
Occupation:	None
Her name means:	"Justice, one who judges"

Background

(Gen. 28:6, 10, 19; 30:21; 31:18, 38; 33:19; 34:1)

Dinah was the only girl in a family with twelve brothers! She was the daughter of Jacob, a rich father, and Leah, a spiritual mother. Her family had moved to Shechem, and Jacob pitched a tent toward that wicked city. Of whom does this remind us? Lot? Shechem was a thoroughfare through the mountains controlling roads to the north and west, a very cultural area.

Reviewing Jacob's travels, we see in his younger years that he left Beersheba to go to Haran. Why? He was fleeing for his life from his brother, Esau, and his father had instructed him not to take a wife "of the daughters of Canaan." Obeying his father, he traveled to Haran. On the way there, he spent the night at Luz. It was there that he wrestled with the Lord and made an altar, renaming the place Bethel. After marrying Rachel and Leah and having a family, God called him back to the land of his kindred twenty years later. However, Jacob did not go all the way back, but stopped at Shechem and bought land from the very people who would deceive him. *(Gen. 33:19)* We see him demonstrating incomplete obedience. Little did Jacob know the catastrophe about to fall upon his family!

Dinah was the only girl, so she may have been spoiled and pampered. Perhaps she was a "tomboy," having only rambunctious brothers with whom to play. She was probably 15 or 16 years old at the time of this move and may have longed for the company of other girls.

Curious, young, daring, and innocent, she wanted to see something of the outside world. The excitement of city life and pretty lights beckoned her. Scripture does not tell us that she asked permission to go into the city of Shechem. Josephus, a Bible historian, says she went to a Canaanite festival of nature worship. She went out unchaperoned, unprotected, and alone!

Tragedy #1 (Gen. 34:2-5, 8; Deut. 22:28-29)

After Dinah arrived in Shechem, the prince's son, also named Shechem, saw her. He lusted for her, took her, and defiled her. Imagine this young girl's bewilderment and hurt! She had only gone to see the city lights and have some teenage fun. Now what would happen to her?

This is the first Biblical account of a rape. Amazingly, God does not spare us the facts in these Bible characters' lives. They are given to us for examples and warnings, the good along with the bad. First Corinthians 10:11 speaks of the Israelites and tells us, "Now **all** these things happened unto them for ensamples: and they are written for our admonition, upon whom the ends of the world are come."

Though Shechem had raped Dinah, he fell in love with her and asked his father, Hamor, to get her for his wife. Hebrew law was later to state this practice. The man was to give the girl's father fifty shekels of silver and then marry the girl. *(Deut. 22:28-29)*

Upon hearing the tragic news, Jacob held his peace. Why? Was he too grieved and astonished to speak? Was he afraid of losing his temper and speaking amiss? Had he given up the authority of his home? Did he feel guilty about the move to Shechem? Remember, this was his only daughter!

The Deal (Gen. 34:6-24; Ex. 22:16-17)

Dinah's brothers were grieved and very angry when they heard the news. They seemingly were more upset about the shame brought on the family name than the sin committed.

Hamor, Shechem's father, approached the family with a resolution. He offered a deal for his son to have Dinah and for Jacob's family to marry the daughters of Canaan. Following Mosaic law, Shechem asked the "Jacob" family for grace and said he would pay them whatever dowry they asked. *(Ex. 22:16-17)* He was determined to have Dinah!

The "Jacob" brothers became deceitful and used religion to cover the diabolical act they had secretly planned. They said they could never give their sister to one who was uncircumcised, that it would be a reproach unto them. They were only concerned about an outward sign, not the condition of Shechem's heart. Striking a deal, they said if every male of the city would be circumcised, they would then give their daughters to them, and dwell with them, and become one people. Being an honorable man, Shechem agreed to the plan, little knowing what he was letting himself in for. Returning to the city, Hamor and Shechem talked to the men. We see through the Scripture that they also practiced deceit. They would embrace the external sign of religion because they were interested in Jacob's riches. How do we see this practiced today?

Many times people appear to be true Christians externally. They know all the right talk, they attend church faithfully, they have the outward appearance, and they hold to strict Biblical standards. However, their hearts are not right with the Lord.

Jesus called these people "whited sepulchres" in Matthew 23:27 and said that though their outward appearance is beautiful, within they are "full of dead men's bones and of all uncleanness." Although the Pharisees appeared righteous to men, they were hypocrites. How about you? Does your inner walk with the Lord match all of your outward talk? Or are you a fake like Shechem, his male friends, and Jacob's sons?

Both sides of this tragic situation had ulterior motives. Simeon and Levi wanted revenge; Hamor wanted Jacob's money. How about you? Do you have ulterior motives in serving or pretending to serve Christ? Do you only serve Him for what you can get out of it? Do you serve Him hoping the other Christians will help you every time you have a need instead of interceding to the Lord on behalf of your own and others' needs? Matthew Henry said, "Nothing secures us better than true religion. Nothing exposes us more than religion only pretended to." Shechem and Jacob's sons were about to be exposed.

Tragedy #2   (Gen. 34:24-31; 49:5-6)

Cooperating with the plan, every male of the town of Shechem was circumcised. On day three, when the pain was at its height and movement was difficult, Simeon and Levi plundered the city and killed all of the men. Were they following an Arab custom, which stated that seduction was punishable by death with the brothers of the girl inflicting the judgment? In any case, they justified themselves and were not even repentant. It seems their motive was not only to clear the family name, but also to better themselves, as they spoiled the city, taking cattle and all that was in the city and field. Not being satisfied with this, they also took everything in the houses, including the wives and children. Simeon and Levi revealed their hearts! Where did Jacob stand in the matter? He never forgave them. In Genesis 49:5, he called them "instruments of cruelty" and self-willed.

Their family reputation was ruined, and Jacob did not confront them about the real issue—their sin against God.

Revival and Reconsecration (Gen. 28:22; 33:18-20; 35:2-5)

What a disruption to Jacob's home! Things would never be the same again! Could they forgive and forget?

God, in His infinite love and mercy overruled evil for good. We know Jacob had made a vow at Bethel in his younger years. He then set up his **own** altar in Genesis 33. God told him to go back to the old landmark, Bethel, and to make an altar there. Jacob and his family needed revival. Jacob finally took control of the situation again and resumed spiritual leadership. He told his whole household to put away their strange gods. (Were these the gods Rachel had taken from her father's house?) Their whole family had become cold and backslidden. It took a tragedy to wake them up and change their lives.

Will it take a tragedy to awaken you and change you and your family's lives? Have you become cold and backslidden? Perhaps you need to return to the old landmark and renew your relationship with Christ. Perhaps you need to relinquish the spiritual leadership of your home to your husband and quit serving the fleshly desires that you think make you happy—the things that leave only a void and cause more discontent.

Conclusions

Although we never hear anymore about Dinah in the Bible, her life serves to offer us many warnings and lessons.

We need to instruct our children about the snares of the world. It is imperative to teach them to take a stand against worldly things, even though the flesh sometimes desires those things. Our own lives should serve as examples to them. Do they see us attending worldly events and going to worldly places? Are we practicing the principle of a separated, godly life? First John 2:15 says "Love not the world, neither the things that are in the world. If any man love the world, the love of the Father is not in him." "Wherefore come out from among them, and be ye separate, saith the Lord, and touch not the unclean thing; and I will receive you." *(2 Cor. 6:17)* Are we teaching our children not to develop an appetite for worldly allurements? We are to be holy because we serve a God Who is holy.

Another lesson from Dinah's life shows us that it is not right to marry an unbeliever to avoid scandal. By doing this, a strong Biblical command is broken. "Be ye not unequally yoked together with unbelievers; for what fellowship hath righteousness with unrighteousness? And what communion hath light with darkness?" *(2 Cor. 6:14)* Jacob and Shechem's deal was wrong and ended up bringing tragedy to all involved.

Once again, Dinah's mistake and Shechem's sin not only affected them. Dinah's whole family became involved and suffered reproach. Shechem's people were slaughtered and plundered! It was a terrible price to pay for a moment of lust!

We should never use religion (our faith) to get something we want. God knows the things we want and need, and He wants to give us the desires of our heart. We "have not" because we "ask not" or we ask amiss and God knows it will not be good for us. *(Jam. 4:2-3)* Therefore, if we have a need, let's simply make our petition to the Lord in prayer.

Another great lesson we learn from Dinah is that we need to know where our children are at **all** times and make them accountable to us. We need to teach our children how to cry out for help in a tragic situation. Where were Leah and Jacob? Did they know Dinah had gone out? Do you know where your children are and what they are doing? Proverbs 29:15b tells us "a child left to himself bringeth his mother to shame." It is unwise to leave our children unsupervised, no matter what their age. The devil knows their every weakness and will tempt them. Notice the Scripture says the shame is to the mother. Leah probably regretted the day she left Dinah to herself. Dinah's purity was sacrificed in a moment of time. Carelessness and lack of supervision exact a heavy toll!

The last great lesson we learn is that tragedy often brings revival! Have you experienced some tragedy lately in your life? God wants to use it to draw you closer to His side. He wants to minister the healing comfort of the Holy Spirit to your heart. Though we never forget great tragedies that hit our lives, they serve to remind us of a great, loving, and compassionate Saviour Who walks with us through the valleys as well as upon the mountaintops. A tragedy should serve to deepen our walk and confirm our faith, not to turn us against the Saviour or to embitter us. God does not promise that we, as Christians, will not suffer. "Behold, I have refined thee, but not with silver; I have chosen thee in the furnace of affliction." *(Isa. 48:10)* However, He does promise that He will never leave us nor forsake us, and He will go with us. "...Fear not: for I have redeemed thee, I have called thee by thy name; thou art mine. When thou passest through the waters, I **will be** with thee; and through the rivers, they shall not overflow thee: when thou walkest through the fire, thou shalt not be burned; neither shall the flame kindle upon thee." *(Isa. 43:1-2)*

What furnace of affliction or tragedy has the Lord brought into your life? Are you a rape victim like Dinah? Have you experienced a broken family relationship? Have you been violated in some way? Did you just receive the doctor's bad report? Are you grieving over the recent loss of a loved one? Do financial woes beset you? Whatever it is, rest assured Christ will take you by the hand and go through it with you! He will not leave you comfortless! "The eternal God is thy refuge, and underneath are the everlasting arms..." *(Deut. 33:27a)* Our "burdens are appointments from God to help us, not hurt us. They draw us closer to Him so we will learn how He can sustain us and carry us through our trials." So, "pitch your cares upon the Lord; He is a good catcher." *(Purcell, p. 160)* "Cast thy burden upon the Lord, and he shall sustain thee: he shall never suffer the righteous to be moved." *(Psa. 55:22)*

Dinah's Roles

1. Only daughter
2. Sightseer
3. Rape victim

Dinah's Character Traits

1. Curiosity
2. Carelessness
3. Daring
4. Innocence

Chapter 3

JEPHTHAH'S DAUGHTER

"A Tragedy In The Making"

Facts	
Husband:	None
Children:	None
Occupation:	Unknown
Her name means:	Name unknown

Background

(Num. 32:29, 40; Deut. 3:13; Judg. 11:1-11, 34; 12:7)

Although little is revealed through Scripture about this young lady, we can discover much about her through the Biblical history of her father. Even though we are never given her name, she is remembered as one of the great Bible heroines. Because of her father, she became an innocent victim of a rash vow.

Her father, Jephthah, was the son of Gilead. The tribes of Gad, Reuben, and Manasseh shared the land of Gilead, a "mountain region east of the Jordan," as their inheritance. Gilead was a beautiful, fertile land with many forest areas. Though it was externally beautiful, it was internally full of wickedness, a gathering place of evildoers. "Gilead is a city of them that work iniquity, and is polluted with blood." *(Hos. 6:8) (Unger, p. 477)* Jephthah's family came from this area.

Though Scripture depicts him as a "mighty man of valor," he had three strikes against him. He was the son of a harlot and an outcast because of his illegitimate birth. In Judges 11:2 his brothers told him he would receive no inheritance from his father's house because of this. Little did this family know how God would mightily use Jephthah. Yes, Jephthah was an outcast just like Moses, Joseph, and David, yet God used all to His glory. Finally, Jephthah kept company with evil and vain men. Perhaps he had no choice as he was an outcast.

We see Jephthah as a type of every converted sinner. He was born in sin just like we are, he was disinherited, and he became a companion of the vain. What a picture of our lot in life! According to Romans 3:23 we are all sinners. Because of that fact, we likewise have been disinherited. Adam's sin drove him out of the garden. We have broken fellowship with our Creator. While in our sinful state, we were companions with the wicked and unwise. Due to this fact, we desperately need the Saviour.

Jephthah pictures the Saviour for us also. His own brothers received him not, just like Jesus Christ. His mother was a harlot and Jesus' mother, Mary, was accused of the same thing. Yet, Jephthah was a mighty man, and Jesus was mighty to perform miracles. Living in Tob, a far country, Jephthah hid himself. Often we find that Jesus sought a secret place, and ultimately He did go to the far country, Heaven. Jephthah gathered worthless fellows together, and Jesus had His disciples do the same thing in Luke 14:21b: ". . .Go out quickly into the streets and lanes of the city, and bring in hither the poor, and the maimed, and the halt, and the blind." Christ gathers vain men and redeems them!

However, in spite of his hard home life, God saw fit to use Jephthah as a judge of Israel for six years. *(Judg. 12:7)* Once again, we see no respect of persons with God. Though Jephthah's brothers had cast him out and wanted nothing to do with him, they were soon to change their minds.

The Ammonites were making war against Israel, and the people needed a leader. His brothers had to grudgingly admit that perhaps Jephthah was the one to call. Jephthah was not readily sympathetic to their call. Hadn't they cast him out? Why did they want him now when they were in trouble? Does God think the same thing about us? When things are going great, do we keep Him on the "back burner," only to retrieve Him when trouble arises? Do we only talk to Him when we are in trouble?

The brothers insisted and wanted to make him their head. According to Judges 11:9 Jephthah seemed to have a relationship with the Lord, as he talked of the Lord and sought Him.

His Rash Vow   (Deut. 23:21-23; Judg. 11:12-31)

Jephthah's brothers made him head and captain over them. Jephthah immediately rose to the occasion and demonstrated great leadership. He was not afraid to confront the Ammonites and asked them whom they thought they were to come three hundred years later and try to take the land. They had oppressed Israel for eighteen years. The Ammonite king refused to reconcile, demanding the restoration of land near Jordan. Jephthah reminded the king that he had denied the Israelites safe passage through the land. Because of this, the Lord helped the Israelites win the land fairly and squarely. The king still refused to hearken, so Jephthah prepared for battle.

Caught up in the excitement of the moment, we see Jephthah making a reckless vow. He told the Lord that if He would deliver the Ammonites into his hand then he would offer Him a burnt offering of whatsoever came out of his house to meet him. Why did he do it? Did he want the honor the elders had promised him? Was he sincere? Was he in the Spirit or just foolish? Was he just "talking big" in front of the boys? He made any promise to ensure victory and seemed to be bargaining with God. God had power to deliver him without this bargaining! He has power to deliver you without bargaining.

Often people with habits will bargain with God. If God will only take away their bad habit, they promise to do this and that for Him. How about serving Him wholeheartedly in the first place? Or if God will help them with their debts, **then** they will tithe. If God will heal them of a dreaded disease, **then** they will be faithful. If God will help them get to retirement, **then** they will attend all the church services. God does not want or need or appreciate our bargaining. He wants us to obey Him from a heart of love, not bargains. Jephthah reaped great heartache due to his bargain with the Lord.

His Return from Battle   (Judg. 11:32-35)

The Lord was faithful to give Jephthah the victory over the Ammonites. Scripture tells us he smote twenty cities, subduing the Ammonites. However, his victory party was to be short-lived. As he returned home, his only daughter came out to meet him, rejoicing with timbrels and dancing.

Immediately, he remembered his rash vow to the Lord. Showing much distress, he tore his clothes and cried out, "Alas, my daughter!" Imagine his feelings at this time! His only daughter! His only hope of grandchildren! But, he was a man of his word and could not turn back from his vow.

How we need to beware of the vows we make to the Lord. A vow is an important thing in the Lord's sight! "When thou vowest a vow unto God, defer not to pay it; for he hath no pleasure in fools; pay that which thou hast vowed. Better is it that thou shouldest not vow, than that thou shouldest vow and not pay." *(Eccl. 5:4-5)*

Enter the heroine of our story.

His Daughter's Response (Judg. 11:36-39)

What a willing and submissive spirit Jephthah's daughter demonstrates in Judges 11:36! She realized the Lord had delivered the Ammonites into her father's hand. Becoming a heroine, she told her father to "do to me according to that which hath proceeded out of thy mouth..." She did not rebel, cry, or "throw a fit!" Manifesting a love for her country and her father, she willingly submitted.   Her one request was to be allowed two months to bewail her virginity.   It was a disgrace to die unwed and childless.   "She gave her life, but retained her honor." *(Deen)*   This precious victim would never know the love of a husband or the joy of children, yet she humbly yielded herself to her authority and the Lord's will.

Jephthah, being a man of his word, intended to keep the vow. This was his only daughter, the only chance he had for continued posterity.   If she did not have children, his name would die. Jephthah learned a hard lesson and probably suffered many troubling thoughts and sleepless nights due to his impulsiveness.

His willing and obedient daughter returned after two months of bewailing her virginity.   How amazing!   She could have run away, but she returned to face her terrible fate!   Scripture says Jephthah "did with her according to his vow." *(Judg. 11:39)*

Interpretations of the Vow (Lev. 20:2-3; 27:28-29; Deut. 21:18-21; Judg. 11:31, 35, 39-40)

Bible scholars do not agree on how his vow was fulfilled. There are two views, one **for** a literal sacrifice, and one **against.** Those **for** a literal sacrifice list the following reasons:

1. They point heavily to the wording of Judges 11:31b
   and 39 --**"I will offer it up for a burnt offering."**
   "...she returned unto her father, **who did with her according to his vow.**
2. The event occurred where heathen dwelt, and human sacrifice was not uncommon.   It was the time of the judges.   Everyone did what was right in his own eyes.
3. It took her two months to bewail it.   Her bewailing was because she would die childless.
4. Jephthah's grief was excessive. *(vs 35)*
5. People usually lament the dead, not the living.   Four days each year, the Israelite women lamented her. *(vs 40)*

However, those **against** a literal sacrifice use several different arguments:

1. They translate verse 31 using **"or"** instead of **"and."**
    For example, what person met him would be dedicated to the Lord's service **or** what beast would be a burnt offering. In view of this, scholars say she remained celibate, living like a nun. However, Scripture does not indicate one is more holy who lives unmarried.
2. The law forbade the sacrifice of children. *(Lev. 20:2-3)*
3. Magistrates had to consent before a criminal child was put to death. *(Deut. 21:18-21)*
4. She remained celibate – "knew no man." *(Judg. 11:39)*
5. Sacrifice involved the priests who would never have participated in human sacrifice.
6. The daughter never bewailed her death, only her virginity.
7. The Bible does not say that he killed her. Her perpetual virginity was the death of Jephthah's lineage.

Whatever the case, Jephthah and his daughter suffered serious consequences due to his rash vow. In spite of this, God saw fit to include Jephthah in His hall of faith in Hebrews 11:32.

Conclusions

What a lesson for us to "be careful little tongue what we say." Our short-sighted faith can get us into trouble, as we often speak before we think. We should be careful what we vow! Jephthah's harm should be our warning. A father's sins have lasting effects on his children. His vow affected not only **him,** but his whole family for years to come. Jesus said, "But, I say unto you, that every idle word that men shall speak, they shall give account thereof in the day of judgment." *(Matt. 12:36)*

The heroine in our story is a great picture of Christ. She was an only child, chaste and pure. She willingly offered herself to her father and was given by her father who loved her. She was willing to give her life as a sacrifice for her people and their freedom from the enemy, the Ammonites. What a wonderful example of submission she is to us!

She did not question her father's will, but humbly followed. Are we humbly following our Father's will today? Sometimes that may involve suffering. Notice that her suffering affected her whole future, not just a day or week of her life. If she lived, she would forever carry the reproach of childlessness.

Precious friend, are you facing days, weeks, or even years of suffering? Perhaps a chronic illness has affected your body and your spirit. Maybe your days are filled with the care of a loved one who is slowly deteriorating before your very eyes. Are the bills mounting up with no way out? Has a fatal accident claimed a loved one? Turn to Jesus, your best Friend. He alone can give peace that the world will never give.

You may find yourself pictured in the lives of many Bible characters. David knew calamity in his own life as he wrote in Psalm 57:1: "...yea in the shadow of thy wings will I make my refuge, until these calamities be overpast." Note he uses the plural form of the word calamities! One burden after another pursued David in his life. Is one burden after another pursuing you?

> 'Sometimes the trials of life seem to come in on us like waves. It seems we just get up again and get our feet on solid ground when another wave of problems comes along and knocks us down. How are we going to stay on top of our problems instead of under them? We must climb higher on the Rock, get closer to Christ.' *(Purcell, p. 172)*

Notice that David went on to state in Psalm 57:7, "My heart is fixed, O God, my heart is fixed: I will sing and give praise." Jephthah's daughter had a fixed heart. Can you sing and praise God through your trial? Is your heart fixed on Him?

What do pain and tragedy bring to our lives? They draw us aside for a time, giving God opportunity to speak in His still small voice. Likewise, God uses them to shape and mold us. Finally, we understand what others are facing, creating a desire to reach out to them in their misery. Therefore, we have a whole new ministry to others because of our own suffering! "The inward work of pain is meant to influence our outward attitudes and actions." *(Jones, "Lights on Main Street," p. 152)* "Who comforteth us in all our tribulation, that we may be able to comfort them which are in any trouble, by the comfort wherewith we ourselves are comforted of God." *(2 Cor. 1:4)* Perhaps Jephthah's daughter was able to reach out to other women who were childless. She understood their anguish and reproach. Can you reach out? Are you able to get out of the "mulligrubs" long enough to recognize that other people, besides you, face great trials also? God wants to use your adversity.

God knew we would face days of trouble and sorrow in our lives. Psalm 50:15 says, "And call upon me in the day of trouble: I will deliver thee, and thou shalt glorify me." Notice the Word does not say, "call upon me **if** you have trouble." It says "**in** the day of trouble." We **will** have troubles and trials, but God has a toll free number. Are you calling on everyone but Him? *(Purcell, p. 135)*

Who would think to pray for suffering? An old Puritan prayer shows that exact plea:

> 'Grant that I may be salted with suffering, with every exactment tempered to my soul, every rod excellently fitted to my back, to chastise, humble, break me. Let me not overlook the hand that holds the rod, as thou didst not let me forget the rod that fell on Christ and drew me to him.' *(Bennett, p. 91)*

May our sufferings – yours and mine – draw us ever closer to our loving Saviour's side. May we, like Jephthah's daughter, willingly and obediently submit to the Lord's will for our lives.

May our sufferings motivate us to reach out to other suffering sisters around us!

Jephthah's Daughter

Her Roles

1. Only daughter
2. Martyr
3. Heroine
4. Patriot
5. Victim
6. Virgin

Her Character Traits

1. Courage
2. Obedience
3. Willingness
4. Innocence
5. Submission

Chapter 4

NAOMI

"The Bitter and the Sweet"

Facts
Husband:	Elimelech
Children:	Mahlon, Chilion
Occupation:	Housewife
Her name means:	"Pleasant," "lovely," or "amiable"

Background

The story of Naomi and Elimelech occurs during "the days when the judges ruled." *(Ruth 1:1)* As you recall from our study of Ruth, *(Women of the Bible, Vol. 2)*, it was a period of time when "every man did that which was right in his own eyes." *(Judg. 21:25)*

Ryrie comments on Ruth: "The book provides a glimpse into the lives of ordinary, though godly people during the turbulent period of the judges. It shows an oasis of faithfulness in an age marked by idolatry and unfaithfulness." *(Ryrie, p. 406)*

Yes, Naomi's family was a godly one, though they made an unfortunate and an unwise decision that would cost them dearly. During her life, Naomi would travel "from a mountaintop existence of bliss into a deep and dark valley of sorrow." *(George, "Women Who Loved God," 5/30)* This godly lady would experience triple heartache and grief, but God in His mercy and grace, would turn her weeping into joy.

Making a Poor Choice (Ruth 1:1-2)

Naomi was married to Elimelech, a godly man, whose name meant "my God is King." Bible scholars believe Elimelech was the brother of Salmon, Rahab's husband, and came from a family of some means. This may have afforded Naomi with a comfortable lifestyle, experiencing no want and having every need met.

Their home was in Bethlehem-Judah, the later birthplace of Jesus Christ. Ironically, Bethlehem-Judah ("the house of bread") was undergoing a great famine. God had brought judgment on the little town due to the disobedience of the Israelites. "A fruitful land is turned into barrenness, to correct and restrain the luxury and wantonness of those that dwell therein." *(Matthew Henry)*

Elimelech had always been able to provide for his family in a great way. Perhaps the famine brought fear to his manly pride. He did not like the uncertainty and inconvenience the future in Bethlehem held. Because of this, he decided to uproot his family and take them to Moab ("waste" or "nothingness"). We do not see him seeking God or counsel concerning his decision. Did Naomi agree with his decision? What about her power of influence? Did their fear of hunger and death override God's perfect will for their lives? Whatever the case, they left a famine of physical food in exchange for a famine of Christian fellowship. What a price they would pay for their decision!

Quick decisions are often unwise decisions. As women, we can coax our husbands into making a wrong decision. Often we become accustomed to good food, nice clothing, pretty homes, shopping sprees, etc. When our husband's job is threatened, and financial fears overtake us, we begin to worry and to complain. Instead of taking our concerns to the Lord and living by faith, we prefer to take matters into our own hands. We may leave a good Bible-believing church (Bethlehem) to go to the far country (Moab) for fulfillment of material needs. Matthew 6:33-34 gives us God's counsel: "**But** seek ye **first** the kingdom of God, and his righteousness; and all these things shall be added unto you. Take therefore no thought for the morrow; for the morrow shall take thought for the things of itself. Sufficient unto the day is the evil thereof." Beware of coaxing or goading your husband into a quick, hasty decision you will all later regret. Instead, become an intercessor and a prayer warrior, waiting upon God for His forthcoming provision and perfect will.

Don't be like Naomi and Elimelech, a "prodigal family" who left their home of plenty to eat out of the "garbage can" in Moab. *(McGee, Vol. 2, p. 90)*

Living in Extreme Distress (Ruth 1:3-5)

The first sorrow Naomi experienced in Moab was the loss of her husband. Remember, she had no pastor or Christian fellowship in this heathen place to encourage her during this time. She was a helpless and hurting woman left to raise her two sons, Mahlon and Chilion, alone. There was no adult male leadership to guide, direct, or provide for her. Perhaps she had to glean in the fields herself to provide a living for her family. The days were long. It was a vicious cycle – go to work, come home, clean, cook, spend time with the boys, sleep – only to be repeated day after monotonous day, and all of this in a foreign country far from home, family, and friends. Whom could this single parent rely upon? She had left all of her relatives and Christian friends! She needed the local church and good godly counsel. She needed other Christians for her boys to emulate. Perhaps she spent many sleepless nights crying out to God.

To add to her sorrow and dismay, we find her sons marrying wives from the Moabite women. What could she expect? It was the only fellowship they knew. They may have been **nice** girls, but they were not **Christian** girls. Perhaps Naomi begged and pleaded with them not to take the step, but it was too late. They had remained in the far country too long. So, she tried to make the best of the matter and win the girls as her friends. Perhaps she shared the stories of the Israelites and all of God's goodness with them.

After ten years of this, more trial was heaped upon her. Both sons died, leaving her totally alone in the foreign country. Grief, loneliness, and fear filled her thoughts. Life was just one big drudgery, each day no different than the one before it. Being a poor widow and having no sons to provide for her, she faced abject poverty. What would she do? Would God provide?

Preparing to Return (Ruth 1:6-18)

Then, all of a sudden she received unexpected news from Bethlehem! "...the Lord had visited his people in giving them bread." *(Ruth 1:6)* How her heart longed for reunion with her kinfolk! With much eagerness, she packed her bags and the little clothing she had. Determining to return to her former homeland, she set out with Ruth and Orpah. How she anticipated seeing her friends and family again! She had missed the Christian fellowship for over ten years.

There may have been another part of her, though, that dreaded "facing the music" from friends who had encouraged her not to leave. Consequently, it would be a bittersweet experience for her to return. However, she was determined to follow through.

> 'Whenever we have disobeyed the Lord and departed
> from His will, we must confess our sin and return to
> the place of blessing. Abraham had to leave Egypt and
> go back to the altar he had abandoned *(Gen. 13:1-4)*;
> Jacob had to go back to Bethel *(35:1).'* *(Wiersbe, p. 152)*

Have you abandoned God's will for your life? Are you still on track in your walk with the Lord or have you taken a detour? Perhaps the detour looked like a better route to you just as it did to Naomi; but, like her, all you have found is bitterness and brokenness. Don't be afraid to confess your mistake and return to have sweet restored fellowship with Christ.

We see the beautiful relationship Naomi had developed with her daughters-in-law. Orpah and Ruth said they would return with her. Naomi then pointed out the difficulties this would cause them. She blessed them for being good wives to her boys, commending them and praying for them. She encouraged them to return to their own homes, pointing out that they were young women, and she had no other sons for them to marry.

Why didn't she encourage them to convert to her religious beliefs? Perhaps she did not want them to make a quick decision they would later deny. She knew it would be difficult for them as foreigners in her homeland.

Orpah turned back to her gods, but Ruth chose the better part and accepted Naomi's God. "It was when Naomi took steps in the right direction herself that others began to be blessed and drawn to the Lord." *(McAllister, p. 105)* Naomi had to separate from the world (Moab) and return to her godly heritage. Only then did Ruth comprehend the years of Naomi's witness to her. The "restored backslider," Naomi, and the "new convert," Ruth, proceeded on their journey to Bethlehem.

Had Naomi's loss brought about Ruth's gain of salvation? Spurgeon wrote:

> 'Naomi had suffered great temporal loss; she had lost her
> husband and two sons; but now she had found the soul of
> her daughter-in-law. . . There ought to have been more joy
> in her heart at the conversion of Ruth's soul than grief
> over the death of her husband and sons.' *(Treasury, p. 595)*

How about you? What is hindering you from fellowship with God's people and the local church? Hebrews 10:25 instructs, "Not forsaking the assembling of ourselves together, as the manner of some is; but exhorting one another: and so much the more, as ye see the day approaching." Do you have wrongs that need to be made right? Is there some sin you need to confess?

Learn from Naomi and be willing to return and "face the music." Don't allow past mistakes, sorrows, or broken relationships keep you from living for God. You may hold the key to someone else's spiritual renewal.

Good things were beginning to happen to Naomi. God had become her first priority. What awaited her in Bethlehem?

Arriving in Bethlehem   (Ruth 1:19-22)

What a stir Naomi's return created! Scripture says "all the city was moved about them" - all the women that is. Can you see the ladies of the town discussing Naomi and Ruth? How their tongues must have wagged about the hottest topic of the day!

Her lady friends barely recognized her. The years of living in a heathen country and the grief and sorrow had taken their toll on her. She herself admitted that her life had gone from pleasantness to bitterness, evidenced in her remark to the women, "Call me not Naomi, call me Mara..." *(Ruth 1:20)* Naomi bore a wounded spirit and carried a heavy load. "The spirit of a man will sustain his infirmity; but a wounded spirit who can bear?" *(Prov. 18:14)* Life's trials had affected her inwardly and outwardly.

Recognizing God's judgment in her life, she said she had left full, but now returned empty. Naomi had faced not only physical starvation, but also spiritual starvation. Her joy had dissipated, leaving a weak, broken, and depressed lady. Like David, she could say, "For I am poor and needy, and my heart is wounded within me. I am gone like the shadow when it declineth: I am tossed up and down as the locust." *(Psa. 109:22-23)*

However, God was about to change her poverty to plenty, her brokenness to completeness, her emptiness to fullness, and her heartache to joy! Full restoration was just around the corner. Naomi was about to experience Psalm 30:5: "...weeping may endure for a night, but joy cometh in the morning." She had taken that first step back to God, and He was waiting with open arms to receive her. By returning to Bethlehem, she demonstrated faith that God would intervene and help her.

How about you, dear sister? Are you a weak, broken, and depressed lady? Have you walked out of God's will and faced spiritual starvation? Does everything else in your life claim top priority **except** the Lord? Are you like Naomi, bound by bitterness? Are you hindered by the past, plagued by the present, and dreading the future?

> 'Disappointment grows into discouragement, which in turn
> spirals down into depression, and even farther into despair.
> Link by self-imposed link, circumstance's chain is formed...
> Ultimately, we put the padlock in place: bitterness.'
> *(Jones, "Lights on Main Street , p. 64)*

God has the key or the combination to your padlock of bitterness. Will you allow Him to free you? Your trial should challenge and change you for the better, not become a yoke around your neck. God offers you complete restoration! He is waiting with open arms to receive you. Won't you take that first step back to Him? Rededicate your life, and give the Lord first place. Allow your chains of bondage to be loosed and obtain freedom of spirit to serve the Lord once again. Watch His restoration begin!

Earning a Living   (Ruth 2:1-17)

Demonstrating resilience and diligence, Ruth wasted no time and took charge of the situation. She realized that Naomi needed someone to look after her and to provide food for the table. Being much younger and physically stronger than Naomi, Ruth set out to pursue a job. God rewarded her diligence by placing her in the field of Naomi's relative, Boaz. Boaz extended grace to the Moabitish damsel, allowing her to glean in his field. Ruth obtained not only provision, but also protection from this kind man.

Imagine her eagerness and joy when she took her gleanings home to Naomi! What a good relationship they experienced! How well they communicated! Ruth explained the whole day to her, and Naomi realized that Ruth was working in her relative's field! What satisfaction she probably felt, knowing they would be well-provided for.

Naomi and Ruth had wonderful fellowship. Each cared for the other. Jealousy did not corrupt their thoughts or deeds. They sought the best for one another. Because of this, Naomi developed a plan for Ruth based upon her customs and experience.

Making a Match   (Ruth 3:1-18)

Looking out for Ruth's well-being and happiness, Naomi asked her if she wished help in seeking a marriage partner. Well aware of the customs and knowing Boaz was the kinsman-redeemer, Naomi instructed Ruth to approach him. She gave Ruth specific details about the approach. Ruth demonstrated a humble spirit and a willing heart. Though she was not familiar with the customs, she submitted herself to her mother-in-law's authority and followed her explicit instructions. Naomi had won her daughter-in-law's heart. How did she do this? Through many years she had shown Ruth love, patience, example, care, and concern. Ruth had witnessed Naomi's testimony during the good times and the bad times. She had seen her human frailties. However, she had also seen Naomi's willingness to admit a mistake and return to her country. Thus, Ruth had the utmost confidence in her.

After approaching Boaz, Ruth returned home to give Naomi a full report. *(Ruth 3:16)* Boaz had sent a gift of barley, showing goodwill and provision for Naomi. Naomi told Ruth to be patient and wait, knowing Boaz must approach the nearer kinsman. Suspecting Boaz's feelings for Ruth, she knew he would waste no time in the matter!

Experiencing God's Grace   (Ruth 4:1-22)

Soon, the business transaction was completed at the gate of the city and Boaz was free to marry Ruth. How Naomi rejoiced! Just imagine her making the wedding plans! Their home would now be complete with male leadership and provision. God had proven Himself to them once again. Her bitterness, depression, and brokenness were gone! Joy had come in the morning!

More excitement pervaded the home when Ruth told Naomi she was with child! Naomi was to be a grandmother! How quickly the news spread throughout Bethlehem. "Did you hear the good news? Naomi is going to be a grandma!" The women of the town blessed the Lord and told Naomi that the grandchild would be "a restorer" of her life and a "nourisher" of her old age. Life once again held promise of good things to come! God had indeed blessed her!

Scripture tells us Naomi took the child into her bosom and nursed it. The neighbor women were so excited that they named the baby, Obed, meaning "servant." Obed was David's grandfather and in the lineage of Christ. The broken years were forgotten, and the scars of the past were dim. Naomi's chains of bitterness were gone, replaced by joy and happiness.

Conclusions

What wonderful lessons we can learn from Naomi's life! She provides an example of things to avoid and of things to pursue. The first lesson we learn from her life is never to encourage our husbands to make a move for money when there is no good church in the area. Wrong priorities! Though we do not see her encouraging Elimelech, we do not see her discouraging him, either. Often, a Christian family will leave a good Bible-believing church to obtain a better job. Seeking a church in the area is not their first concern. They get to the far country and realize there is no Christian fellowship in the area. Beware!

Though she became broken in spirit, we see Naomi exhibiting humility and bravery in returning to Bethlehem. The lesson we learn is: Do not be afraid to "face the music." Return to God and be restored!

The demonstration of a beautiful mother-in-law/daughter-in-law relationship is clearly seen throughout the story. What a challenge for us to emulate!

The story of Ruth and Naomi portrays many of God's attributes for us. He is a God of provision, a God of grace, and a God of mercy! He waits for us to call upon Him! He wants first place in our lives!

We also see God sustaining Naomi throughout her infirmity, throughout the helpless and hurting years. He carried her through grief, the loss of a loving husband and two sons. He upheld her and encouraged her when Ruth accepted her God.

Though Naomi faced severe testing and trial, she kept her heart **fixed**. "O God, my heart is **fixed**; I will sing and give praise, even with my glory." *(Psa. 108:1)* "He shall not be afraid of evil tidings: his heart is **fixed, trusting in the Lord.** *(Psa. 112:7)* She knew where to go for help.

How about you, dear friend? Is your heart fixed on the Lord and the things of the Lord? Prayer and your own personal walk with God will either help you endure your affliction, remove the affliction, or "transform the trouble into triumph." *(Wiersbe, p. 307)* Naomi's trouble was transformed into triumph, but not right away. She endured her testing for many years.

Are you allowing your circumstances to get the better of you? Are your troubles hindering your walk with the Lord or drawing you closer to His side? Let me encourage you to take it to the Lord! He desires for you to live a victorious Christian life and wants to transform your trouble into a glorious triumph. Keep your heart fixed on Him, the Author and Finisher of your faith!

Naomi's Roles

1. Wife
2. Mother
3. Mother-in-law
4. Grandmother
5. Nurse
6. Teacher
7. Matchmaker
8. Widow

Naomi's Character Traits

1. Determination
2. Humility
3. Kindness
4. Courage

Chapter 5

HANNAH

"The Woman with a Prayer Life--
The Intercessor"

Facts	
Husband:	Elkanah
Children:	Samuel, five unnamed children
Occupation:	Housewife
Her name means:	"Grace, favor, gracious, graciousness"

Background

Our story opens in Ramathaim-zophim, also known as Ramah, a town located approximately two hours northwest of Jerusalem. Here we find Hannah, another brokenhearted woman. Like Sarah, Rebekah, and Rachel, she bore a heavy burden of barrenness. Remember the importance of childbearing and what a stigma barrenness carried! First Samuel 1:5 tells us the "Lord had shut up her womb," showing us that the ability to have children comes from the Lord. If you recall, when God saw that Leah was hated, He shut Rachel's womb. *(Gen. 29:31)* Women who were barren experienced great grief of mind and soul. "The woman's kingdom was the woman's family. . . Her empire was her motherhood." *(Matheson, p. 196)*

Not only did Hannah face a burden of barrenness, but she also lived during a time of stressful conditions:

1. **Political stress** – It was the time of the judges and
   there was oppression from neighboring countries.
2. **Religious stress** – There was corruption in the priesthood
   and she would soon be misunderstood by her pastor.
3. **Family stress** – She faced polygamy, jealousy, and
   being misunderstood by her husband.

What would Hannah do? To whom could she turn for help?
Was there any help?

Her Family and Faith   (1 Sam. 1:1-8)

Hannah was the wife of Elkanah, a man who feared and
loved God. To add fuel to the fire of barrenness, Hannah had to
share her husband with another woman, Peninnah. We see the
turmoil this double marriage brought into the home. It mirrors
the same relationship seen with Sarah and Hagar and that of
Rachel and Leah. However, we will see Hannah respond
differently to her trial than Rachel and Sarah did to theirs.

The "Elkanah" family was a worshipping family and went
yearly to Shiloh to sacrifice to God. Though Hannah shared her
husband, Scripture tells us she was the favorite wife as he
lavished more upon her. This probably created envy and
jealousy between the two women. Had Hannah, like Sarah and
Rachel, encouraged Elkanah to take another wife due to her
barrenness? Scripture does not tell us, but we do know that
Peninnah had several children. First Samuel 1:6 reveals that
Peninnah tormented Hannah over this situation, and the torment
was merciless. "And her adversary also provoked her **sore**, for
to make her fret…" It is interesting to note in 1 Samuel 1:7, the
pronoun changes to "he" perhaps denoting the fact that Satan
used Peninnah in this matter. "And as **he** did so year by year . . .
so she provoked her." Hannah lived out David's words in Psalm
119:86: "…they persecute me wrongfully; help thou me."

We do not know how long this occurred, but 1 Samuel 1:7 says "year after year." Apparently, Hannah's torment was ongoing for several years. She lived in emotional turmoil and depression. Facing sleepless nights and restless days, her appetite waned, and finally she did not eat at all. The yearly journey to Shiloh that should have been a happy family outing became a miserable trip for her. "We ought to take notice of our comforts, to keep us from grieving excessively for our crosses." *(Matthew Henry)* Her barrenness had become her main focus, though it does not appear that she tried to avenge herself with Peninnah. Elkanah loved her so much and asked if he was not better to her than ten sons? *(1 Sam. 1:8)* After all, he gave her everything a woman could want, **except children**.

Her Petition and Promise (1 Sam. 1:9-18; Rom. 8:26)

Hannah knew Whom to seek in her distress. She did not run all over town and share her heavy burden with others. After all, they could not help. Even her husband could not give her the comfort she sought.

> 'The greatest hindrance to our spiritual development – indeed, the whole hindrance - is that we allow our passions and desires to control us, and we do not strive to walk in the perfect way of the saints. When we meet the least adversity, we are too quickly dejected and we turn to other people for comfort instead of to God.' *(Kempis, pp. 11-12)*

Perhaps she had sought God time after time before, but she was not about to give up. We see the beautiful example of imprecatory prayer in her life. She ran to God with her problem and finally put her focus in the right place! Lockyer said, "Her pain found a refuge in prayer." After the sacrifice had been offered and eaten, she took refuge in her Lord. Scripture points out her vexation of spirit. First Samuel 1:10 says, "And she was in bitterness of soul, and prayed unto the LORD, and wept sore."

Notice her approach to the Lord in 1 Samuel 1:11: "And she vowed a vow, and said, O LORD of hosts, if thou wilt indeed look on the affliction of thine handmaid, and remember me, and not forget thine handmaid, but wilt give unto thine handmaid a man child, then I will give him unto the LORD all the days of his life." Notice her approach:

1. She was very **selfless** and vowed to give God her son.
2. She was very **specific** in her request.
3. She was very **submissive** and used the term "handmaid."
4. She was very **stubborn** – **"continued praying."**

What a lesson to us in persistent prayer! Have you ever been that burdened down, dear lady? Perhaps you are like that even this day as you read about Hannah's life. Then, like Hannah, cry out to the Lord to remember you and to help you with your problem. Be specific and persistent in your request, submitting yourself unto the Lord! He is waiting for you to run to Him for comfort and has the answer to your dilemma.

Lacking compassion and having never witnessed this type of praying, preacher Eli thought she was drunk. He could see her lips move, but he heard no sound. The custom of the day was to pray audibly and in a voice that could be heard. Long prayers and loud voices were "in." (Remember the Pharisees in the New Testament?) However, Hannah prayed silently and internally, reminding us of Romans 8:26: "Likewise the Spirit also helpeth our infirmities: for we know not what we should pray for as we ought: but the Spirit itself maketh intercession for us with groanings which cannot be uttered." Eli asked her how long she would be drunk and instructed her to put away her wine. Imagine Hannah's embarrassment. No one understood her!

'It was difficult enough that she cried herself to sleep every night because she had no child; worse yet that her insensitive husband expected her to be satisfied with him only, yet married a second wife so he could enjoy having children; and even worse that the second wife tormented her day after day because of her barren-ness. But then her spiritual leader, the high priest, accused her of alcoholism and idolatry. Had even God forsaken her? *(Handford, Women Under the Judges, p. 77)*

Hannah collected her wits and explained the situation to her preacher. She told him she was not drunk, but sorrowful in spirit and thus had poured her soul out to the Lord. Notice she did not reveal her innermost pain of barrenness, though she did plead with him not to consider her a wicked woman or a daughter of Belial, a worthless person.

Although Hannah had been falsely accused, she demonstrated respect to Eli and called him "lord." A drunk certainly would not do this! Eli told her to go in peace and said the God of Israel would grant her petition.

Hannah left in peace. She had given her problem to the One Who would settle it for her. Scripture tells us she ate and was no longer sad. Her internal prayer had brought internal peace. God gave her a "garment of praise" for a "garment of heaviness." She had faith and trusted Him to answer. Although Hannah could not rejoice in her circumstances, she could rejoice in the Lord of her circumstances. *(Purcell, p. 300)* Her ongoing situation and everyday circumstances were no longer going to enslave her. She was once again the old Hannah, happy in her heart and free in her spirit!

Dear lady, what is keeping you all bound up in your spirit? Have you allowed your everyday circumstances and ongoing trials to give you tunnel vision? God is waiting for you to fall on your face before Him in prayer. Cry out to Him in faith, believing and knowing He alone has the answer. Then wait patiently for Him to provide.

Her Prayer Answered   (1 Sam. 1:19-23)

God did not forget Hannah's burden. After returning home from their yearly journey to the temple, the LORD remembered

Hannah and she conceived. Imagine her joy and happiness! She was finally experiencing what other women had experienced. Comparing notes with her pregnant friends, outgrowing her normal clothing, choosing a name – all of these things brought great joy to her mother's heart. Imagine her excitement and joy when she experienced the first movement in the womb! What a dream come true this was! With great anticipation and eagerness, she awaited the birth of her baby.

Hannah lovingly named him Samuel, meaning "name of God." She remembered her promise and told Elkanah that she would give him for the Lord's service after he was weaned. She took her motherhood seriously and would not make the yearly trip to Shiloh. Perhaps she was still recovering, and she knew she would not have much time with the little one. She nursed the child and was very dedicated to motherhood. Elkanah respected her judgment in the care of the child. What a miracle God had provided! The tumultuous home was now one of peace!

Her Promise Fulfilled (1 Sam. 1:24-28; 2:18-21; 2 Chron. 31:16; Eccl. 5:4-5)

Unlike some who make promises, Hannah kept her promise to the Lord. After weaning Samuel, she dedicated him to the Lord's service. Although we are not sure of the exact age, some speculate that it was between three to seven years. Imagine her feelings! She may have experienced joy and pride at fulfilling her vow mingled with sadness and tears in leaving her first-born child. Perhaps her previous trials had prepared her for this day! Whatever the case, we never see her demonstrating a begrudging spirit. She realized the blessing had come from the Lord and willingly lent her son back to Him. "All of our gifts to God were His first gifts to us." *(Matthew Henry)* Her gift to the Lord was for Samuel's whole life. She was leaving her son on a mission field. What a beautiful example of self-sacrifice Hannah is to us! She so aptly depicts the Lord's grace in the giving of her only son. Will we give our children to the Lord for service or do we discourage them from full-time Christian work? What promise have **you** made to the Lord that you have not kept?

Hannah visited Samuel every year and took him a hand-made coat. He saw his mother's faithfulness to church and her love for the things of the Lord. Can the same be said of you? Is it obvious to your children that you love the Lord and delight in His service? Eli told her she would have more children. However, Hannah did not know this before she took Samuel to the temple.

God rewarded Hannah's faithfulness by giving her five more children, three sons and two daughters. *(1 Sam. 2:21)* Her home rang out with the laughter of young voices and the noise of running feet. However, there was always a special place in her heart for that firstborn.

Her Praise and Thanksgiving (1 Sam. 2:1-11; Luke 1:46-52)

Though Hannah's heart may have been sad after leaving her son, we see her offering firstfruits of praise to God. She praised God before she even knew she would ever have other children. We see her song in 1 Samuel 2:1-11. Her praise came from a heart full of gratitude and was directed to the Lord, not to the preacher or Samuel. "What we win with prayer we must wear with praise." *(Matthew Henry)* Through her song of praise we see several of God's attributes in 1 Samuel 2:

1. His holiness	*(vs. 2)*
2. His omniscience	*(vs. 3)*
3. His omnipotence	*(vs. 4-8)*
4. His provision and protection	*(vs. 4-8)*
5. His preservation	*(vs. 9)*
6. His judgment	*(vs.10)*

Her song offers the first mention of the "anointed," portraying her not only as a poetess, but also as a prophetess. It has been called the "forerunner" to Mary's Song in Luke and is very similar to it. *(Cp. 1 Sam. 2:1, 4-6 to Luke 1:46-47, 51-52)*

Conclusions   (Gen. 18:12-13; 25:21; 30:1; Acts 3:24)

Hannah exhibited many godly qualities and was a "lily among thorns." She was tenderhearted toward the Lord and demonstrated self-control. Though she was childless, she was not prayerless, and she sought refuge from the Lord during the bad times. She maintained a heart full of praise and gratitude. Her reaction to her trial was vastly different from that of other Bible ladies. Sarah laughed, Rebekah appeared indifferent, Rachel was irritable, but Hannah took it to the Lord!

Like Jochebed and Mary, she gave her son to the Lord's work and slipped into the background. Her success was in the life of her son. The Bible mothers who had children in the "limelight" were obscure. They just patiently trained and instructed, happy to see leaders made of their sons.

Her son's list of accomplishments brought great joy to her mother's heart. Samuel worked alongside Eli in the temple. He anointed King Saul and King David. He was the first prophet and the last of the judges. God thought him important enough to include in the Hebrews hall of faith. *(Heb. 11:32)*

Lessons from Hannah's life show us the necessity of guarding our tongue and self-control. We also witness God's great comfort in time of sorrow. Hannah demonstrates selflessness in offering her son for service to the Lord. Scripture uses no negative word about Hannah. What a lady of faith she was!

Lastly, we learn from Hannah's life the importance of faithful, fervent prayer and turning to God instead of to others for help. "Suffering from what she did not have, precious Hannah grabbed onto what she did have – the rope of prayer – and drew herself and her situation up to God's heavenly throne." *(George, "Women Who Loved God," 6/4)*

God was always there for Hannah and He is still there for you today! If you are helpless and hurting, apply the lessons from Hannah's life, and allow the Lord to minister to your spirit. Then, share those lessons with another friend, encouraging her along the way. Remember, "faith that cannot be tested cannot be trusted. God tries our faith, not to destroy it, but to develop it." *(Wiersbe, p. 325)* Last of all, don't forget to praise and thank the Lord for His benefits and blessings in your own life.

Hannah's Roles

1. Mother
2. Wife
3. Intercessor
4. Seamstress
5. Poetess
6. Prophetess
7. Song-writer

Hannah's Character Traits

1. Unselfishness
2. Self-Control
3. Humility
4. Gratefulness
5. Godliness
6. Patience
7. Persistence

Chapter 6

RIZPAH

"The Grieving Widow"

Facts
Husband:	Saul, Abner
Children:	Armoni, Mephibosheth
Occupation:	Concubine
Her name means:	"Hot or live coal, a hot or baking stone"

Rizpah is a name synonymous with suffering and personal tragedy. She faced greater tribulation than any other Old Testament woman. Becoming a victim of vengeance during a time "of national strife and war," we see her demonstrate a passion for her family not often seen in others. Learning about her life is like reading a diary of tremendous grief and overpowering woes. Who was this lady? What happened to her?

The Tainted Past   (2 Sam. 3:7-11)

We are given a short biographical sketch of Rizpah in 2 Samuel 3:7. She was the daughter of Aiah and one of Saul's many concubines, "a secondary or inferior wife." Concubines were often obtained to raise heirs for their master. Upon Saul's death, Scripture implies that Abner, Saul's general had an adulterous relationship with Rizpah. This was a "treasonous act, for it was in essence making a claim to the throne." *(Ryrie, p.470)* Saul's oldest son, Ishbosheth, was heir to the throne, so he confronted Abner about the matter. Abner was astonished that Ishbosheth could think he would be a traitor to Saul, and

Scripture tells us that Ishbosheth dropped the matter because he feared Abner. So, we see Rizpah's diary open with turmoil and struggle.

The Troublesome Days (Gen. 9:6; Num. 35:31, 33; Deut. 24:16; Josh. 9:18-21; 1 Sam. 20:15; 2 Sam. 21:1-7)

War continued between the households of Saul and David for many years. David "waxed stronger and stronger, and the house of Saul waxed weaker and weaker," until Saul died, and God finally promoted David to rule over the entire kingdom. *(2 Sam. 3:1)* Several years later, severe famine struck David's kingdom. After three years of famine, David inquired of God the reason. God told him it was because of Saul and the oath he had broken with the Gibeonites, which Joshua had made five hundred years before. It is interesting to note that God keeps a record of our vows and promises. The sowing and reaping principle was now taking effect.

Joshua had promised the Gibeonites that he would not destroy them – they could live peacefully among the Israelites as "hewers of wood and drawers of water." *(Josh. 9:20-21)* Saul had broken this promise, thereby incurring God's future judgment on Israel. God even called Saul's house a "bloody house."

David asked the Gibeonites how he could atone for this. The Gibeonites did not want money, but vengeance or blood ("an eye for an eye, a tooth for a tooth"). They demanded justice and sought a severe penalty. They refused to leave it in God's hands. The only thing that would satisfy their wrath was the deliverance of seven of Saul's sons to be hanged. Saul's sons may have been involved with the prior slaying of the Gibeonites. *(2 Sam. 21:2)*

What could David do? He agreed to the proposition, but spared Jonathan's son, Mephibosheth, due to an oath he himself had previously made. How would this affect the concubine, Rizpah?

The Terrible Tragedy (Ex. 20:5; 1 Sam. 31:8-9; 2 Sam. 3:30; 21:8-9)

Imagine David's grief over such an ordeal! Rizpah had presented Saul with two sons. Scripture tells us David took Rizpah's two sons, Armoni and Mephibosheth, plus Michal's five sons, and he gave them to the Gibeonites. Could this have been God's judgment? Saul had promised Merab to David, but then gave her to another man. Scripture intimates that Rizpah had been involved in an adulterous relationship. God will only tolerate sin so long!

The Gibeonites killed and hanged the seven young men at the beginning of barley harvest (mid-April). Imagine Rizpah's feelings! She had already lost two husbands, Saul and Abner. Having no male leadership in her home, these sons may have been her only reason for living, and now they had to pay the price for someone else's sin. Do you think she asked why? It was not fair! She faced overwhelming circumstances. However, "God's Word repeatedly assures us that our places of overwhelming are His places of undertaking." *(Jones, "Wilderness," p. 17)*

The Triumphant Vigil (Ex. 20:5; Deut. 21:22-23; 2 Sam. 21:10-14)

In order to assuage her intense grief and to honor the dead, Rizpah took sackcloth, a symbol of mourning and penitence, sat on it, and protected the bodies of her sons from vultures and wild animals. She kept this vigil in the heat of the day and the cold of the night! Day after day and night after night she demonstrated her heart of love!

> 'What a ghastly scene that must have been during barley
> harvest with those seven blood-covered bodies hanging on
> the respective trees, and noble Rizpah protecting them
> from the vultures waiting to gorge themselves on the
> corpses!' *(Lockyer, p. 143)*

She did the only thing she could do – she gave the only thing she had left to give! People probably thought she was crazy! She did not give any thought to her own comfort. She had a cause! What incredible suffering and sacrifice are shown!

How long did Rizpah do this? "...from the beginning of barley harvest until water dropped upon them out of heaven." *(2 Sam. 21:10)* Ryrie states, "From the barley harvest of April to the early rains of October, Rizpah protected the exposed bodies from scavengers." Most Bible scholars agree that this vigil lasted five months, while some say it may have been a few days until it rained. The rain pictures God's withdrawal of His judgment.

Rizpah faced this sorrow all alone. The only thing she had left was God. She reminds us of Hagar who faced her sorrow alone in the wilderness. However, we do not know if Rizpah believed in God, because we do not see her cry out to Him or call upon Him.

Leaving the men unburied shows us this was a deed of vengeance because the law stated anyone hanged on a tree had to be buried before sunset. *(Deut. 21:22-23)* The curse was fulfilled, and Saul's sons were an example to all.

David received word of Rizpah's vigil. His heart was stirred enough to give the seven sons a decent burial. Scripture says he buried them in the sepulchre of Kish, Saul's father. Rizpah's vigil had paid off. Her sons received an honorable burial.

Conclusions (Rom. 5:3-5; 8:18)

Rizpah's life was full of grief, but she did not allow it to immobilize her. Showing great determination and love, she stood by her sons not only in life, but also in their deaths. Sorrow became her constant companion. Have the companions of sorrow and grief immobilized you? Dear lady, if you know Jesus as your Saviour, you have the comfort of the Holy Spirit readily available and waiting for you. Why not tap into that comfort and peace?

> 'For every trial that God's people have, there are exceedingly great and precious promises of help. Some of you have laid awake worrying about things that God has already answered in His Word. You are like a person in the dark who is dying of hunger while locked in a kitchen. There is food all around if only you would put out your hand and take it. Child of God, if you search the Scriptures, you will find that the Master has opened the pantry of promise.' *(Spurgeon)*

Claim God's promises of comfort for your own life and share them with other hurting people.

Notice that Rizpah gave her all. Giving helps take the focus off ourselves and our problems. One author has said, "Giving unlocks our own hearts to God's comfort." Do you want to experience the comfort of God? Then, give to others. Allow sorrow to stretch your heart. Rizpah's giving stirred the heart of a king. Who knows how our selflessness will affect others?

Rizpah's sons were a symbol of Jesus Christ. They were innocent, they were hanged on a tree, and they paid for the sins of others.

Rizpah went from a queen's garments to sackcloth. We never know the trials we will face in this life! She was an innocent bystander suffering the consequences of the troubled days of war in which she lived.

Is there not a cause for us as Christian ladies, wives, and mothers? Can we be modern-day Rizpahs and chase the vultures of the world away from our own children - vultures of wayward friends, wrong music, and wicked enticements like drugs, immorality, pornography, etc.? Can we give our all for Jesus?

If you have tasted of sorrow and grief, who is better than you to help another lady in her time of despair? Be there for someone else! Make that phone call, bake that cake, or write that note. Someone needs you to be a "Rizpah" in her life today. Put that arm around someone.

Rizpah's Roles

1. Mother
2. Concubine
3. Widow
4. Protector
5. Adulteress?

Rizpah's Character Traits

1. Unselfishness
2. Determination
3. Patience
4. Devotion
5. Perseverance

Chapter 7

TAMAR
"Victim of Incest"

Facts	
Husband:	None known
Children:	None known
Occupation:	None known
Her name means:	"A palm tree"

Background

Once upon a time there was a young lady named Tamar. Her name meant "palm tree" picturing for us a beautiful and stately form. Scripture pictures her as fair, chaste, and ambitious. *(2 Sam. 13:1, 18)* The palm tree is known for many uses, especially its fruit and its juice. The fruit of the palm tree, the date, is called *tamr* in Arabic. *(Fallows, Vol. III, p. 1632)*

With Tamar's life like a fairytale existence, the stage was set for only good things. She was the daughter of King David and Maacah. Luxurious housing, excellent food, and beautiful clothing filled her days. She knew no want and had older brothers at her beck and call. Everything was going so well, until sin entered the picture.

The Wrong Friendship   (2 Sam. 13:2-5)

Tamar had an older brother named Amnon who was heir to David's throne. What could he possibly want or have need of? He, like Tamar, had everything. However, it does not appear that he had a walk with the Lord. Perhaps materialism ruled his life. The more he obtained; the more he wanted. Amnon developed a lust for his sister, Tamar. He dwelt on his impure thoughts day and night. His lust was unnatural, forbidden, and wicked. The flesh warred against the spirit, even causing lack of appetite and weight loss. His lust became a physical distress to him as a "rottenness of the bones."

Amnon had a cousin, a friend named Jonadab. Scripture tells us he was a "subtil man," cunning and crafty. He asked Amnon what was wrong with him. Amnon revealed his wicked thoughts about his half-sister, Tamar. Jonadab, eager to please and wicked himself, devised a diabolical plan for Amnon. He asked Amnon, "Aren't you the king's son? Can't you have what **you want?** I'll help you get it!" A godly and true friend would have been shocked and abhorred at Amnon's thoughts. It was not so with Jonadab. He was a base man and perverted, just like Amnon.

What kind of friends do your children have? Remember the old adage, "You become like those you run with." Scripture even teaches us in 1 Corinthians 15:33 that "evil communications corrupt good manners." You may be diligently teaching your child God's Word and keeping him in church, but allowing him to run with a wrong friend. Beware! That wrong friend will destroy all the good things you have so patiently been teaching him. Sometimes as ladies we are so merciful and afraid of hurting someone's feelings, so we allow a friendship that should not be. Do not sacrifice your child because you fear hurting others. Ask the Lord to give you boldness mixed with grace and tact to sever that friendship. Remember, you are the one who allowed it to develop in the first place!

What kind of friends do **you** have? Do your friends encourage you in your walk with the Lord or pull you down? Are you able to discuss the Scriptures and edify one another, or does your talk consist of worldly amusements and material goods? Evaluate your friendships.

Amnon's wrong friend, Jonadab, told him to pretend to be sick and to ask his father to send Tamar to minister to him by making some cakes. Amnon fell for the plan, thinking only of himself and his wicked desires.

David went to see his son, and Amnon followed through with the lie. Bible scholars agree that God hid Amnon's evil intentions from David's discerning spirit. David was about to reap the consequences of his sin with Bathsheba. God had promised judgment, and judgment would come! David's sin affected his whole household, the guilty and the innocent.

The Sinful Tragedy   (2 Sam. 13:6-14)

Not suspecting anything adverse, Tamar went to Amnon's house and made him the cakes he requested. However, he refused to eat them and ordered all the servants and men present to leave. He then ordered Tamar to take the cakes to an inner chamber. When Tamar entered the room, Amnon took hold of her and asked her to lie with him.

Some authors blame David for Amnon's actions, as David lived a double standard before his children. "Parents know not how fatal the consequences may be if . . . they give their children bad examples." *(Matthew Henry, Vol. II, p. 507)* What a lesson to us as mothers and grandmothers! Children repeat what they see and hear us do. Are you living a reputable testimony before your children? Do they see God as first priority in your life, or have you let worldly desires pervade your home? David's sin was ever before him in the lives of his own family.

Tamar strongly resisted and attempted to reason with her lust-driven brother. She called him "brother," reminding him of their relationship. She told him the act was expressly forbidden. Naming the act for what it was, she besought him not to force her or commit such a great "folly" (sin). She told him it would bring shame to her, and he would be as a fool in the land. Continuing her frantic pleading, Tamar suggested perhaps the king would allow them to marry. However, none of her arguments prevailed, and Amnon carried out his dastardly deed.

The Emotional Consequences (2 Sam. 13:15-21)

The prevailing emotions were anger, hatred, hurt, shame, humiliation, degradation, and desolation, to name a few.

> 'It's no wonder a woman feels that rape is the ultimate degradation. It isn't just the physical dangers of death and disease, though those are terrifying; it's the sense of helplessness, of violation of the inner person, the defiling of that most holy of human relationships.'
> *(Handford, Women Under the Kings, p. 35)*

Amnon's self-gratifying lust turned to hatred. Scripture states "he hated her exceedingly." In fact, the hatred was so great that he ordered his servants to put her out and lock the door. His own sinful act had become odious to him. He knew he carried the blame; however, he did not have a humble heart or a penitent spirit.

Tamar begged him not to put her out as it "would inevitably be supposed that she had been guilty of some shameful conduct herself." *(Unger, p. 1251)* She was a broken, pathetic woman. The hurt was so deep and the helplessness so far-reaching. Rending her beautiful garment and applying ashes to her head, Tamar went on her way crying. She sought shelter with another brother, Absalom. He asked her if Amnon had been with her and seemed to know what kind of man Amnon really was. He then told her not to tell because it was a family issue. She remained "desolate" in Absalom's house. Some authors think she remained single the rest of her life, though we hear no more of her after this terrible incident.

Although Absalom appeared calm outwardly, inwardly he was seething with anger and a spirit of hatred. He wanted total revenge and planned a later assassination attempt. His root of bitterness grew worse and worse, as he waited for two years to take any action. The fruit of David's sins had not all ripened, yet.

How did David feel? He was "very wroth." Although angry, like Eli and Samuel, he did nothing to discipline or restrain Amnon. Perhaps he remembered the judgment Nathan had pronounced on his household. What a price it was to pay! The whole family was in turmoil, and Amnon's sin was covered.

Matthew Henry states that after this tragic occurrence, a law was made stating "a young man and a young woman should never be alone together..." since even a king's daughter had been violated. *(Henry, Vol. II, p. 509)* According to Old Testament law, Amnon was worthy of death. *(Deut. 22:25-26)*

The Family Division   (2 Sam. 13:22-39)

Amnon sowed the wind and reaped the whirlwind and destruction. *(Hos. 8:7; Prov. 1:26-27)* Two years later, Absalom carried out his vengeful plot by inviting the family to a feast and having Amnon murdered. Where was Amnon's good friend, Jonadab? He told David not to worry or take it to heart because it was only Amnon who had died and no one else! Great division ruled in the family, and Absalom went into hiding for three years!

Imagine David's feelings! Although his earlier life "was full of music and dancing, the latter part had far more of mourning and lamentation in it." *(Spurgeon, Treasury, p. 722)*

And what of Tamar? She carried the scars of hurt with her the rest of her life. Absalom named his daughter after her. We are not told if she ever experienced joy or happiness in her life, but God, the great God of justice and mercy, says, "Vengeance is mine; I will repay saith the Lord." *(Romans 12:19b)* He has a way of balancing the scales in His perfect timing.

Conclusions

Though Scripture remains silent concerning the remainder of Tamar's life, her sad, shameful story offers us many lessons and reminders to help us in our lives as ladies of today.

First, it is important whom we choose as friends. Do your friends lift you up and edify the Lord? Do you feel refreshed after being with them, or do you feel guilty about the conversations you have had and the things you have done? Your friendships should strengthen your walk with the Lord. It is good to have planned things to do with your friend like visiting a shut-in, working in a church ministry together, or cooking, baking, sewing, and canning together. Share what you have been learning in your devotions, and ask your friend what she has been learning. Choose godly friends and make sure your children do the same.

Secondly, are you a testimony to your children or are you living a double standard before them? Are your speech and actions the same at church and at home? Although David was considered the apple of God's eye, he lived a double standard bringing judgment upon his entire family.

It seems that Tamar was an innocent victim of a diabolical scheme. Perhaps she had no walk with the Lord. We do not see her crying out to the Lord even in her day of distress. If she did not have a walk with the Lord, she likewise had no spiritual discernment. It did not seem odd to her that Amnon would send all the men out or call her into the inner chamber. To whom could she turn in her time of tragedy? – only a family member who was carnal and deceiving himself. What a lesson for us to maintain discretion and not to be alone with someone of the opposite gender!

Dear lady, do you have a walk with the Lord? Have you accepted Him as Saviour and Master of your life? To whom do you turn when trials and sorrow come your way? Perhaps, like Tamar, you have been an innocent victim of a terrible crime or deed. Only the Lord Jesus Christ can bring you inner healing and peace of mind after such a tragic event. Apply the balm of memorized Scripture to your heart. Replace the fearful and hateful thoughts with verses like Philippians 4:7-8, 2 Corinthians 10:4-5 and Psalm 139. Create a soothing atmosphere in your home by playing good Christian hymns and music. Reach out to others even in your own distress, taking your focus off your own problems. Pray and seek God like you never have before. The God of all comfort is waiting for you with open arms. *(2 Cor. 1:3)* Allow Him to restore you spiritually, physically, mentally, and emotionally.

Remember that Jesus, like you, was the victim of an innocent crime, and even during that crime, He was thinking of others. There **is** healing, peace, and joy for you again! Take one day at a time, and claim the victory over your tragedy! "He will revive us where we feel dead, resurrect us when we feel low, and renew and enlarge us in our spiritual life. *(Wiersbe, p. 341)*

Tamar's Roles

1. Princess
2. Sister
3. Cook
4. Victim

Tamar's Character Traits

1. Obedience
2. Ambition
3. Purity
4. Gullibility
5. Lack of discernment

Chapter 8

THE WIDOW OF ZAREPHATH
"A Helpless Widow, A Hospitable Woman"

Facts

Husband:	Deceased
Children:	One son
Occupation:	Homemaker
Her name means:	Name unknown

Background

The nation of Israel was once again experiencing God's judgment due to its sinful ways and wicked rulers. The prophet Elijah had just experienced a triumphant victory over Ahab, Jezebel, and the prophets of Baal. He had predicted a great drought in the land. Following these events, God directed him to the brook of Cherith for rest and refreshment (a little R&R). The brook eventually dried up, and God told him to go to Zarephath, a city in Zidon.

Zarephath was a seacoast town, northeast of the Sea of Galilee, along the Mediterranean, known for its "purple dye, olive oil, metal goods, and pottery." *(Ungers, p. 1378)* Zidonians were also known for their handicraft. They produced beautiful embroidered robes and silver bowls. Their ships were well known as the best in Xerxes' armada. *(Fallows, Vol. III, p.*

1750) Archaeological excavations have also revealed that the inhabitants of the town worshipped Tanit and Astart, goddesses of fertility.

It was in this atmosphere, this heathen town, that God, in His great love and mercy, had already prepared the heart of a widow lady to care for Elijah. What is so amazing about this? Elijah was to find refuge in the homeland of his worst enemy, Jezebel. Plus, how was a poor widow going to take care of him? Why didn't God send him to a rich widow? Certainly God's ways are not our ways!

Although we never learn her name, we do learn some valuable lessons and insights from her life. She is a type of the Gentiles to whom Elijah was the first prophet sent, a widow with "an empty cupboard and a dying son." *(Deen)*

The Discouraged Widow (1 Kgs. 17:10-12; Mark 9:41)

Times were lean, and days were discouraging for this widow lady. Not only was she experiencing a dire famine, but she also had lost her husband and therefore had no one on whom to lean. As Elijah approached the gate of the city, the widow was "there" gathering sticks. She had no firewood or fuel with which to even cook a meal! What depth of poverty and misery she faced! Apparently there had been no inheritance, as this lady could not even afford a servant. She was just going about her daily routine when Elijah appeared. The Lord placed her right in his path.

Elijah asked her for a drink of water. This became her first small test of faith since the country was in a drought. At this point, she may not even have realized that Elijah was a man of God. She asked no questions nor gave any excuses but acted immediately upon his request. As she turned to go, he made another request for bread.

The poor widow honestly explained her situation telling Elijah she had only a handful of meal left and a little oil. She spoke of Elijah's God as the "LORD thy God." She and her son were at the point of starvation. Her son is mentioned for the first time. Imagine how discouraged and downhearted they were! Perhaps her son had already become so weak that he could not even help her look for or gather sticks for their last meal. Elijah had come to this town to be ministered unto, but he himself was going to minister to this woman!

The First Test (1 Kgs. 17:13-15; 18:1; Heb. 13:2)

The prophet told her not to be afraid, but to bake him a small cake first. Imagine the thoughts that went through her head! What about her son? This man looked healthy! This was a test of faith for her. The test concerned her present, physical needs. Elijah promised her she would have enough meal and oil until the Lord sent rain. How long would this be? What did she have to lose? After all, her gods and goddesses were not helping!

Scripture tells us "she went and did according to the saying of Elijah." *(1 Kgs. 17:15)* Elijah's faith was contagious. She heard and acted upon what she heard. What an example of faith and obedience she is to us! She put action to her faith in Elijah's words. Demonstrating hospitality, she entertained an angel unawares. *(Heb. 13:2)*

The First Miracle (1 Kgs. 17:15-16; 2 Cor. 9:8-10)

According to the Scripture, they all ate many days. God proved His power of abundance and provision to her – just like the manna in the wilderness and the water to wine at the wedding. (He promises us day by day our daily bread.) His promise was fulfilled. The barrel remained full of meal and the cruse full of oil. Did she run and keep peeking into the barrel and pot? Notice that her reward was greater than her service. She baked one cake for the prophet and was repaid with many. Like the widow who gave the mite, this poor widow is an example that God is looking for a giving heart, even among the poor. There is no outgiving the Lord! "By her obedience, she exchanged the uncertain for the certain, famine for plenty, death for life." *(Harrison, p. 331)*

Spurgeon interprets this passage to mean the "barrel never filled, and yet it never emptied. The store was little, but it was always sufficient for the day." *(Spurgeon, "Treasury," p. 776)* Likewise, he taught that the Lord continued to give her just enough for every meal. Why could this be so?

1. If others heard she had a store of meal, they would have wanted it also, perhaps robbing her and killing her.
2. Meal will not keep in great quantities; it becomes wormy.
3. It induced her to continue her pleadings with God and taught her a daily dependence upon Him.

> 'So long as we have a full barrel of our own merits, God will have nothing to do with us. So long as the cruse of oil is full to overflowing, we shall never taste of the mercy of God. For God will not fill us until we are emptied of self.'
> *(Spurgeon, "Treasury," p. 775)*

Though her nation had provoked the Lord, the Lord demonstrated great love and mercy to her by His provision.

The Second Test   (1 Kgs. 17:17-20)

Because the widow manifested faith in her trial, the Lord wanted to take her another step. Her son became very ill and died. Hadn't she already been through enough? How could God do this to her? Now she had no one! Imagine her anguish and despair. It seems this was her only child. Why was he saved from famine only to die now? What did the future hold for her?

Her faith wavered even though she had seen the miracle of the oil and the meal. Isn't that just like us today? We see God work great miracles in our lives only to resort to confusion and doubt when the next trial arrives. She thought she was being punished for some sin in her past. Perhaps she was under conviction. Had she been involved in Baal worship? The country was known for it! She became helpless and bitter, questioning Elijah. The valley of dark despair overshadowed her.

Elijah never answered her, but picked up the boy and took him to his room. Crying out to the Lord, Elijah put the whole situation before Him. He knew Whom to approach in the hour of crisis. The widow's extremity became God's opportunity to manifest Himself to her again.

The Second Miracle (1 Kgs. 17:21-24)

What an example of intercessory prayer we see through Elijah. He stretched himself upon the child and cried again, pleading with God for the child's life. God heard his prayer and revived the child, demonstrating His great healing power. The death of the child was for the glory of God. Elijah then took him back to his mother. This seems to be the turning point for the widow. She now admitted Elijah was a man of God, and the words he spoke were the words of the LORD.

So it is with our lives. No testing – no growth! Our trials often drive us to the Word and to our knees. She was chosen for the "furnace of affliction" to deepen her faith. Like the widow of Zarephath, our circumstances become a window through which we see and believe in God.

> 'To a praising saint, the circumstances of life are a
> window through which he sees God. To a complaining
> saint, these same circumstances are only a mirror through
> which he sees himself.' *(Wiersbe, p. 122)*

The widow of Zarephath became a praising saint! She came to know that her Creator would be as a husband to her, loving, caring, and providing for her every need. "For thy Maker is thine husband: the LORD of hosts is his name; and thy Redeemer the

Holy One of Israel; the God of the whole earth shall he be called." *(Isa. 54:5)*

This biography affords great comfort to widows of today. God has promised never to leave nor forsake you. His grace is sufficient for each new day.

Conclusions (Luke 4:25-26)

What rich lessons we learn from the widow of Zarephath! God's omnipotence and provision are shown throughout. She was the first Bible woman to have her son restored to life. God demonstrated His grace by extending His mercy to a Gentile heathen woman. We see similarities between her and Rahab. Both were heathen, both helped men of God, both exhibited faith, both trusted in the Lord, and both were spared.

Attention was focused on **what** the widow did rather than **who** she was, as her name is never mentioned. God thought her actions important enough to include her in the New Testament in Luke 4:25-26, stating that though there were many widows in Israel, Elijah was sent to the widow in Sarepta. Thus, her faith and works are commended. She portrays how sharing with others greatly enriches one's own life.

> 'Is thy cruse of comfort failing?
> Rise and share it with another:
> And through all the years of famine
> It shall serve thee and thy brother.
>
> Is thy burden hard and heavy?
> Do thy steps drag wearily?
> Help to bear thy brother's burden –
> God will bear both it and thee." *(Lockyer, p. 203)*

God honored her obedience, and her rewards far out-weighed her service. How our heavenly rewards will far out-weigh our service for the Lord here! Someday we will be able to look on

His face and cast our crowns at His feet. What a joyful day that will be!

Has your "furnace of affliction" or your window of suffering and grief enabled you to draw closer to the Lord? Or have you become bitter, complaining, and stalemated in your Christian walk? Allow God to care and provide for you as He did the widow of Zarephath. Perhaps He wishes you to minister to the man of God – your preacher, your Sunday School teacher, your bus captain. Will you find some way to encourage others? Take your two little sticks (what provision you have), and bake a cake for (be a blessing to) the spiritual leader in your life. The widow never lived to regret Elijah's request, although she did not completely understand it at the time. She was "there" when Elijah needed her. Can you be "there" for someone else?

The Widow of Zarephath

Her Roles

1. Wife
2. Mother
3. Widow
4. Servant
5. Sustainer
6. Provider

Her Character Traits

1. Obedience
2. Ambition
3. Hospitality
4. Generosity
5. Cooperation
6. Selflessness

Chapter 9

THE SHUNAMITE WOMAN

"A Great Woman"

Facts

Husband:	Name unknown
Children:	One son
Occupation:	Homemaker
Her name means:	Name unknown

Background

Scripture shares with us another biography of an unnamed lady. This lady lived in Shunem and was known as "a great woman." Great may have referred to her rank and position, her riches and wealth, or her nobility and age. Whatever her greatness, we will discover that she was a gracious and godly lady, ministering to others, despite her own trial of life.

Although she carried a heavy burden, she never made it known or talked about it. Little did she know how the Lord would reward her for her gracious hospitality, only to have that reward snatched from her in a moment's notice. After experiencing suffering and grief, she would become the recipient of a great miracle.

The Need-Meeter   (2 Kgs. 4:8-10; Prov. 31:20)

Preacher Elisha had just received Elijah's mantle and was beginning his ministry. In his travels, he passed through the town of Shunem, a fertile area located east of Megiddo, "overlooking the valley of Jezreel." *(Ryrie, p. 565)* Arriving in the town, we are told he met a "great woman" who "constrained" or highly encouraged the weary traveler to stop, eat, and be refreshed. Elisha enjoyed this gracious woman's hospitality, and we learn from Scripture that he stopped at her house every time he passed through Shunem. Her home became an oasis to the prophet.

She and her older husband *(2 Kgs. 4:14)* enjoyed the prophet's fellowship and looked forward to his visits. Showing great discernment and perceiving that Elisha was a man of God, she approached her husband with a great idea! Having the gift of mercies, she realized Elisha's need for privacy, rest, and study.

The Bible shows us what a submissive woman she was in her appeal to her husband. Notice that she did not take things into her own hands! She said, "Let **us** make a little chamber," not "**I** am going to do it without seeking counsel from my husband." Perhaps she considered the expense involved with the construction and furnishing of such a room. She enlisted her husband's support and used the words, "I pray thee" in her appeal. Throughout her petition, she used the word **us.**

> "Let **us** make a little chamber, I pray thee, on the wall;
> and let **us** set for him there a bed, and a table, and a stool,
> and a candlestick: and it shall be, when he cometh to **us**,
> that he shall turn in hither.   *(2 Kgs. 4:10)*

What a godly example for us as ladies to follow – a soft, undemanding approach, an explanation of the wish or desire, an inclusion of **him** in the plans, a consideration of **his** feelings, and an acceptance of **his** final decision.

How is your approach to your husband in making an appeal? Do you take his feelings into consideration and value his judgment? You should, because God has set him over you as the authority and head of the home. Often we think our husbands are obstinate or inconsiderate, when we really just want our own way all the time. Just as God sometimes say "no" to our requests, so our husbands look out for our well-being by saying "no." May we learn the approach of a "great woman" and apply it to our own lives.

We do not see her husband deny the request. It seems they may have worked together on this project. What a joy to serve together! They put a bed, a table, a stool, and a candlestick in the room, just the necessary items the man of God would need. Keeping their hospitality simple, they offered a prophet's chamber to Elisha each time he passed their way. Because they sowed good seeds of simple hospitality, they were about to reap a great reward.

The Unmet Need (2 Kgs. 4:11-17)

During one of Elisha's visits, as he lay upon the bed in the little chamber, he called his servant, Gehazi, to come to him. He told Gehazi to bring the woman to see him. Expressing great gratitude and concern for her, he asked her what could be done for her, as she had been such a blessing to him. What a beautiful picture of a grateful heart he demonstrated! "Those that receive courtesies should study to return them. It ill becomes men of God to be ungrateful or to sponge upon those that are generous." *(Matthew Henry)*

The dear lady did not want to be noticed, nor did she expect any reward for her service. What a true servant's heart she had! Showing contentment and humility, she said, "I dwell among my own people." Elisha even offered to mention her name to the king or the captain of the host.

Elisha persisted in his quest to bless her. Gehazi knew of the woman's need and revealed it to Elisha. The "great" lady was barren and had no hope of a child, as her husband was old. Elisha called her again into his presence and told her that she would embrace a son within the next year. Long ago she had given up hope of motherhood, and she begged the prophet not to lie to her or give her false hope! She had been disappointed so many times!

Much to her delight and that of her husband's, she conceived and bore a son! God rewarded her for her servant's heart and her humble spirit. "She built the prophet a room; God built her a house." You just cannot out give the Lord!

The Sudden Death   (2 Kgs. 4:18-21)

What joy rang throughout the "great woman's" house! She lovingly cleaned sticky fingerprints off the mirrors and muddy footprints off the floors. Favorite meals were prepared, and family times were special. Her heart sang with joy as she taught her little boy stories and songs about God. As the lad grew older, his daddy took him along to the fields to help. Imagine the great fellowship father and son had throughout the day!

One day, as they were in the fields, the lad became ill and complained of his head hurting. Daddy sent him with a servant back to the house to his mother. Mom gathered him on her lap and comforted him. At noon, all of a sudden, the boy died in her arms. Only those who have lost a child can relate to the grief and sorrow this lady experienced! A "dream come true" had now turned into a tragic nightmare. How they had loved this child!

Although we see no outward expression of grief, her inner spirit was hurting and broken. She took the lad to the prophet's room and left him there. It is interesting to note that she made no preparation for burial, but for a resurrection. Had she heard the news about the widow of Zarephath's miracle? Was her faith expecting a similar miracle?

The Demonstration of Faith (2 Kgs. 4:22-30; 1 Chron. 23:31; Matt. 9:13; Heb. 4:16)

The "great lady" demonstrated great faith. There was no 911, no urgent care facility, and no EMS. What would she do? She approached her husband and asked him to have a servant get her a donkey so she could **run** to the man of God. It appears that she did not even share the tragic news with her husband. He questioned her trip, but she told him: "It shall be well." Although it was not presently well, she knew it would all work out for the good. Her husband did not exhibit as great of faith, though, of course he did not even know the problem! It was not the normal time to approach the man of God – not a Sabbath, a new moon, or a feast.

We once again see her communicating with her husband and letting him know where she was going. She went through the right channels and again manifested a submissive spirit.

The servant came with the donkey, and the "great woman" saddled her own mount, instructing the servant to lead the way and to stop for nothing. She was determined to reach Mt. Carmel and wanted to waste no time in the matter! Her mission of mercy had consumed her!

Elisha saw her approaching and told Gehazi to go and see what she wanted. She refused to reveal the problem to Gehazi, only stating again, "It is well." Did she discern that Gehazi had a lack of faith? She was so intent on her purpose that when she came near Elisha, she grabbed him by his feet.

What a great example to us! First, this Shunamite woman manifested great persistence and ran to find Elijah. She did not waste any time in getting to the one who **could** help her. By grabbing his feet, she showed she was not about to be denied. Oh, that we would have that same boldness to approach the throne of grace in our hour of need – to "grab hold" of God's promises in the same way! She did not run all over the neighborhood bemoaning her fate or asking everyone else to pray for her. She, herself, was in tune with God and knew where her help lay.

Is your slate clean that you can run to the Saviour at any hour of the day or night? Do you even know what promises from God's Word are yours to claim – provision, protection, guidance, help in trouble, refuge, strength, etc.?

Gehazi was impatient and tried to turn her away. Was he trying to protect his master, or was he unconcerned about her problem? Elisha rebuked Gehazi, realizing the problem was a serious one. He said her soul was vexed, and the Lord had hid it from him. From the depths of her anguished heart, she asked the prophet, "Did I desire a son of my lord? Did I not say, do not deceive me?" *(2 Kgs. 4:28)*

Elisha gave Gehazi his staff and instructed him to go and lay it upon the face of the child. This did not satisfy the woman, as she refused to leave the prophet. Perhaps she realized that Gehazi's faith was not as great as that of Elisha's, and remember, Gehazi had tried to turn her away. Elisha finally yielded to the lady's persistent pleading and went back with her.

Her Faith Rewarded   (2 Kgs. 4:31-37; 5:26-27; 2 Cor. 3:6)

Gehazi ran on ahead, obeying Elisha, but perhaps not from a pure heart. We do not see him pray or seek God on behalf of the child. He had the method, but not the faith. There was no effect on the child. Do we have the method and not the faith, or the heart for our ministry? Are we serving merely out of duty, or because we think others expect it of us? How easy it is to get caught up in such a routine! We volunteer for something because our friends volunteered. Where is our heart in our service? Are we like Gehazi, just running to perform, and not seeking the Lord to empower us? If so, we, like Gehazi, will see little or no effect in our service. Later, the Bible revealed Gehazi's greedy spirit when he took money and goods as a reward for God's miracle in

Naaman's life. *(2 Kgs. 5:26-27)* Gehazi was a hireling who used method for reward, but demonstrated no faith.

What a difference it made when Elisha, the godly, praying prophet came on the scene. Unlike Gehazi, Elisha persisted in method **and** prayer. Faith **and** works!! He sought God alone, realizing the power was not in his staff, but in prayer. Wanting to teach Gehazi a lesson, he portrayed 2 Corinthians 3:6, showing it is not the letter of the law, but the Spirit. First, he prayed, then went in and lay upon the child. After that, he walked around in the house, probably praying again, then repeating the process. The little lad began to sneeze, demonstrating life again! What a miracle!

Spurgeon likens the sneezes of the lad to the beginning of spiritual life in a new believer. Though a sneeze is short-lived, still it **is** a sign of life. A sneeze is unpleasant, unmusical, and monotonous. New believers are awakened to the fact of their unpleasant past, and often they are melancholic and heart-broken about their sin. They ask many repetitive questions and rehearse their confused and chaotic pasts. Like Jesus, we should demonstrate a heart of patience and passion for our new brothers and sisters in the Lord. "We are not examining them for the ministry, we are only looking for evidences of spiritual life." *(Spurgeon, Treasury, p. 842-843)* Can we be a good listener, pray with them, and help them take their next step?

Elisha presented the child to his mother, and she gratefully "fell at his feet, and bowed herself to the ground." *(2 Kgs. 4:37)* The "great woman" always showed respect and a grateful spirit to the man of God. With much joy she gathered her son to her bosom and left. What a happy ending! However, her life's trials did not end here, and the Bible reveals more disappointment to follow.

Further Trial   (2 Kgs. 8:1-6)

As Elisha continued to use his prophet's chamber, he stayed in contact with the "Shunamite" family. One day he told the lady that the Lord was going to send a famine to the area for seven years. He instructed her to take her household and go to another area to live. The lady went to the country of the Philistines.

After the famine, she returned to Shunem, only to discover that she no longer had a home or land. Imagine her heartache and dismay – no place to live, no plot for a garden, nothing! Once again, her determination comes into view. Her family and home were of primary importance to her. Using a bold, but respectful, approach she went to the king to beg and plead for her house and land.

We notice God's providence in the whole matter, as Gehazi had been talking with the king. The king was asking him about the great things Elisha had done. Of course, the greatest miracle was the lad being restored to life, so Gehazi had to share that! Just as he spoke, the woman and her son approached the king! Gehazi told the king this was the very woman! "The woman was by God's wonderful and gracious providence brought thither in the most advantageous season." *(Poole, p. 732)* Responding to her heart's cry, the king told his servant to restore everything – her home, her land, and even the fruit of the field for the past seven years! How merciful God was to her! He provided a second miracle of restoration - first her son, then her home!

Conclusions

What a "great lady" for us to emulate! The Shunamite woman met another's need without even thinking of or mentioning her own. She demonstrated a contented heart and a grateful spirit, desiring to serve God right in her own home and with her own possessions. She received a prophet in the name of a prophet and likewise received a prophet's reward. *(Matt.*

10:41) By providing an oasis spot for Elisha, she later received an oasis herself. What a fantastic example of victorious, Christian living she is to us!

How did she keep a positive attitude in her negative life situations? She knew where to find help! She knew Whom to run to. Her submissive and respectful spirit rendered her due benevolence from her authorities. She did not just take matters into her own hands, but sought spiritual guidance and counsel. After obtaining that counsel, she acted upon it. What a wise, tactful, and balanced lady she was!

Elisha protected his reputation and hers. He always approached this woman through his servant and did not become overly familiar with her. Likewise, the woman from Shunem kept her distance and knew her place. She communicated with her husband.

Her life provides us with many lessons. This lady faced barrenness, the death of a child, famine, and loss of her home and property. Yet, she remained calm throughout all of her trials. This was a great positive trait for her. She did not let her problems keep her from serving God, nor her emotions rule. Self-pity had no place in her vocabulary or actions. She remained determined not to focus on her problems, but when a problem did arise, she immediately sprang into action to solve it.

The widow of Zarephath's and this woman's life closely parallel one another. Both had miracles of restoration, and both were unnamed. Both received **more** than they had given. Both demonstrated hospitality to men of God, and both showed great faith! Although both experienced sorrow while serving, God did not leave nor forsake them, but rewarded their great faith.

Like the songwriter of old, you may be asking, "Does Jesus Care? Does God know what I am going through?"

> 'Does Jesus care when my heart is pained
> Too deeply for mirth and song;
> As the burdens press, and the cares distress,
> And the way grows weary and long?

O yes, He cares – I know He cares!
His heart is touched with my grief;
When the days are weary, the long nights dreary,
I know my Saviour cares.'   *(Frank E. Graeff)*

Rest assured that He does know and care and will come on the scene at just the right time.   Petition Him, beseech Him, get godly counsel, and then act on your faith.   Be a "great woman" of God and for God.

The Shunamite Woman

Her Roles

1. Wife
2. Mother
3. Hostess
4. Servant
5. Need-meeter
6. Intercessor

Her Character Traits

1. Patience
2. Contentment
3. Hospitality
4. Perseverance
5. Kindness
6. Initiative
7. Boldness
8. Balance
9. Submission
10. Tactfulness

Chapter 10

THE SYROPHENICIAN WOMAN

"A Jewel in a Dark Place"

Facts	
Husband:	Unknown
Children:	One daughter
Occupation:	Housewife
Her name means:	Unknown

Background

Though the Bible does not tell us her name or her family's name, God highly commends this Gentile woman for her faith. Scriptures give us a brief glimpse into her life and the adversity and tribulation she experienced. Her account is included in the two gospels of Matthew and Mark. We will see Romans 5:3-4 enacted in her life. "And not only so, but we glory in tribulations also: knowing that tribulation worketh patience; And patience, experience; and experience, hope:" Perhaps you will be able to relate to this "jewel in a dark place."

The Place   (Matt. 15:1-20; Mark 7:1-23)

Our story begins after Christ had just finished a debate with the scribes and Pharisees over tradition versus faith. The religious leaders were all upset that Christ's disciples were not washing their hands before eating bread. These leaders were taking a religious tradition meant only for the priests and expanding it to include others. *(Ryrie, p. 1365)* Jesus pointed out the core of the problem when He told them they were honoring Him with their mouths, but their hearts were far from him. *(Matt. 15:8)*

After this debate, Christ, for the first time since beginning His ministry, stepped out of Israel. He ministered in His hometown of Nazareth, then departed to a desert place and went to a mountain to pray. After performing miracles in the land of Gennesaret, and perhaps being disgusted with His own people, He "departed into the coasts of Tyre and Sidon." *(Matt. 13:54-15:21)*

Tyre and Sidon were seacoast cities in Phoenicia along the Mediterranean Sea. Sidon was the oldest capital of Phoenicia and was a place of Baal worship and other Canaanite cults. "Philosophy, art, and astronomy" were the main skills practiced by the Sidonians, and the people were very wicked indeed. Jezebel, one of the most-wicked women to ever live, was a daughter of Ethbaal, "king of the Sidonians." *(New Ungers, p. 1193)* Tyre, like Sidon, depended much on the seacoast for trading purposes. Its most important product was purple dye made from mollusks. The Canaanite cults also invaded this city, and the prophet Ezekiel denounced the wicked lifestyle of this "worldly wise city." *(New Ungers, p. 1312)*

These cities provide the dark background for our bright jewel of a lady.

The Problem (Matt. 15:22-24; Mark 7:25-26)

Our jewel was a heathen, a Gentile from Tyre and Sidon. Perhaps all she had known her entire life were idol worship and the worldly ways of these two cities. Matthew calls her "a woman of Canaan," and Mark calls her "a Greek, a Syrophenician."

This poor lady was desperate, as she had a very sick daughter with an unclean spirit. Imagine how distraught she must have been! Day after day she had to listen to her daughter's rantings and ravings with no relief in sight. Perhaps she had to sit up at night with the child to make sure she did not harm herself. She needed help! The Bible tells us that as Jesus passed her way, she cried out to Him and besought Him, even falling at His feet. How did she know Whom to seek in her distress? Perhaps she had heard good reports about Him and His other healings. This was probably the first time she had ever seen Him, but she did not wait for a formal introduction. Her problem was so overwhelming that she threw herself on Christ's mercies. Notice that she recognized Him and called out to Him, "O Lord, thou son of David." *(Matt. 15:22)* Already we begin to see signs of her faith. She did not go into a detailed account of her problem. She only begged for mercy and help.

What an example to us! Are you facing an overwhelming situation in your own life right now? Why not cry out to the One Who can help you? Recognize Christ for Who He is. He is able to help with any trial or adversity you are experiencing. In fact, He **wants** to help and is **waiting** for your call.

The disciples wanted nothing to do with this woman because of her nationality. This seemed to be a pattern in their thinking which the Lord constantly had to rebuke. They did not like the Lord taking time for the woman at the well in John 4 or for the little children. *(Matt. 19)* Not seeing an answer to the dilemma, they preferred to send the 5,000 home. *(Matt. 14:15)* They did not like being bothered or inconvenienced, or perhaps they were looking out for their Master's rest! However, Jesus always had patience with people. He told his disciples that He had not been sent only to the "lost sheep of the house of Israel." *(Matt. 15:24)*

What a wonderful lesson to us! God is no respecter of persons. Our position in life, our background, our skin color - none of these things matter to Him. He died for everyone. If this woman had been intimidated by her past, she would never have gone to Him. However, we see her taking that first step of faith which was soon to change her whole life.

The Pause (Matt. 15:23; Mark 7:24)

Much to her dismay, Christ remained silent. Why? This was so unlike Him.

1. Was He trying her faith? (as He did Abraham? Jacob?)
2. Was He weary from His travels and needing rest?
3. Was He testing His disciples' feelings?
4. Was He teaching us to persevere?

It was during this pause that the disciples made their plea to send her away. Matthew Henry said, "Every accepted prayer is not immediately an answered prayer." Have you ever prayed and the heavens seemed like brass? It is hard to be persistent during such a time. How great was this lady's faith!

The Pursuit (Job 13:15; Matt. 15:25-27; Mark 7:25-28; Phil. 3:2)

This jewel of a woman was persistent and not about to be put off! Notice her approach! She could have become angry, but she did not. Scripture reveals three things she did:

1. She **worshipped** Him – fell at His feet. *(Mark 7:25)*
2. She **petitioned** Him, **besought** Him, and **pleaded** with Him, saying, "Lord help me." *(Mark 7:26)*

How did she want help?
   a. If His grace was only to the Jews, she needed help. (She was a Gentile.)
   b. Perhaps she was begging for grace – for help to increase her own faith.
   c. Maybe she was begging for the child's healing.
3. She told Him her **heart** and did not hide her feelings.

Whatever the case, she did not give up!

Christ seemingly rebuffed her and told her the Jews should be fed first. Gentiles were called dogs; however, the Jews were also called dogs later in Philippians 3:2.

This lady rose to the occasion. Can't you just see her squaring her shoulders and preparing for her defense? She defended her own faith and asked if she wasn't at least entitled to some of the crumbs. Even dogs get to eat crumbs from their master's table! Wasn't she as good as a dog? What a great communicator she was, quick-witted, but not disrespectful.

Admitting her own unworthiness, she agreed with Jesus in Matthew 15:27. Since she knew she had no way of helping herself, though, she persevered. She did not ask for special changes to be made for her. She wanted only the crumbs. What discernment and hope she manifested! Christ had come to Tyre and Sidon to preach, right? Wasn't she entitled as a dog under the table to eat? What a smart lady she was! Again she recognized and reverenced Him as Master saying, "the master's table." Previously she had called Him Lord and "Son of David."

She knew that even masters feed their dogs, even though the dogs do not get the children's bread. Dogs were considered foul creatures in the East, and adults had nothing to do with them. However, the children did play with the little dogs, and adults tolerated them in the house for the children's sake. She likened herself to a little dog. Children loved to feed their dogs under the table. His children (disciples) were full. They had His presence all the time. Surely they would not mind her having some

crumbs! It is through the children that dogs are fed! (missions?)
There is enough for all. This is a king's table not a poor man's
table. This lady did not let the discouraging remarks from the
disciples deter her. "Faith can find encouragement even in that
which is discouraging." *(Matthew Henry)*

The Praise   (Matt. 15:28; Mark 7:29-30)

What would Jesus do? He rewarded her persistent faith by
healing her child. He told her, "O woman great is thy faith: be it
unto thee even as thou wilt. Her daughter was made whole from
that very hour." *(Matt. 15:28)* It was an "absent cure" that
showed His instantaneous power. Imagine her joy when she
returned home and gathered the child into her arms! How glad
she was that she had gone to see the Jew! Her patience and
persistence amid tribulation reaped great dividends! Christ
praised her faith. Notice that He was not afraid to compliment
her. Once again we see our Lord's tender, loving compassion for
women. He cares about our problems!

Her faith had remained despite silence, refusal, and reproach.
She put the negative words of the disciples out of her mind.
Perhaps her friends had discouraged her also and told her she
was crazy for going to see that Jew. She did not let depression
overtake her and would not allow her emotions to rule! Her
strong faith triumphed and conquered. Her persistence paid off.

Conclusions

How about you? Are you facing what seems to be an
overwhelming and intolerable situation? Are you persistent and
persevering? Or do you let others discourage you? Be
encouraged to throw yourself at Jesus' feet and beseech Him for
help. "The effectual fervent prayer of a righteous man availeth
much." *(Jam. 5:16)* "Be careful for nothing; but in every thing
by prayer and supplication with thanksgiving let your requests be

made known unto God." *(Phil. 4:6)* Remember, He **wants** to help and is **waiting** to help. Do not be controlled by your emotions and what others say. God is in control and willing to intervene on your behalf.

The Syrophenician woman knew how to make a plea. Perhaps you are facing a trial with someone in authority over you – a teacher, an employer, your husband. Learn from this lady how to make an appeal. She approached the Saviour with reverence and respect for His position. Remaining calm and determined, she stated her case. She did not become defensive or use tears to get what she wanted. She was not afraid to speak up, yet retained a good spirit.

Another lesson learned from this Biblical account is that we should never discourage anyone from coming to Christ because of our own impatience or inconvenience. A soul could be hanging in the balance because of our hasty reactions. Don't hinder folks from coming to Jesus.

Can we, like this jewel of a lady, let our afflictions drive us to Christ? Are we able to intercede for our children - to throw ourselves on the mercies of the Lord in any situation?

Are we able to defend our position in Christ so that others may see and be influenced? How well do we know our position in Him through the Word? What a noteworthy lady the Syrophenician woman was! May we take the lessons of faith from her life and apply them to our own hearts.

The Syrophenician Woman

Her Roles

1. Wife
2. Mother
3. Intercessor
4. Communicator
5. Gentile

Her Character Traits

1. Determination
2. Unselfishness
3. Persistence
4. Patience
5. Discernment
6. Humility
7. Courage

How to Order

(Give a gift to your friends, Pastor's wife, teacher, relatives, or students and save $ in quantity.)

Additional copies of this book are available by mail.
Use the order form below and send to:

Starr Publications
740 Jefferson Lane
Red Lion PA 17356
www.Starr-Publications.com

Bookstores—Write and ask for a special discount Bookstore Order Form.

Clip, Complete, and Send with your check or money order

Order Form

Please send me:

Qty.	Title	Cost each	Total
_____	*Women of the Bible, Vol. 3 Helpless & Hurting*	$ 6.60	$_____
_____	*Women of the Bible, Vol. 2 Faithful & Fruitful*	6.60	_____
_____	*Women of the Bible, Vol. 1 Helpmeets & Homemakers*	6.60	_____
_____	*Dress—The Heart of the Matter*	6.60	_____

Subtotal A (add) $_____

Less Discount for Quantity   (circle one)......... -_____

3-6 bks 10%   7-12 15%   13-18 20%   19-45 25%   46-75 33%   76+ 36%

Subtotal B   (subtract) .... $ _____

Add Shipping & Handling in the U.S.A. by US Postal Media Mail + _____

1-3 bks $ 2.60   4-6 $ 3.10   7-9 $4   10-12 $5
13-16 $5.40   17-22 $.37 ea.   23-51 $.29 ea.   52+ $.26/bk

Order Total (include check or money order for...) $ _____

Please send book(s) to:
Your name _____
Mailing Address _____
City, ST, Zip _____
Phone # for questions _____

Send to: **Starr Publications**, 740 Jefferson Lane, Red Lion PA, 17356

Sources

Bennett, Arthur, ed. *The Valley of Vision.* Carlisle, Pennsylvania: The Banner of Truth Trust, 2002.

Chappell, Clovis G. *Feminine Faces.* Nashville: Abingdon-Cokesbury Press (Whitmore & Stone), 1942.

Davis Dictionary of the Bible. Nashville: Royal Publishers, Inc., 1973.

Deen, Edith. *All of the Women of the Bible.* New York: Harper and Row Publishers, 1955.

Deen, Edith. *Wisdom From Women in the Bible.* San Francisco: Harper and Row Publishers, Inc., 1978.

Fallows, Samuel. *The Popular & Critical Bible Encyclopedia, Vol. I, II, and III.* Chicago: The Howard-Severance Company, 1907.

George, Elizabeth. *The Remarkable Women of the Bible.* Eugene, Oregon: Harvest House Publishers, 2003.

George, Elizabeth. *Women Who Loved God.* Eugene, Oregon: Harvest House Publishers, 1999.

Handford, Elizabeth Rice. *Profiles of Genesis Women.* Chattanooga: Joyful Christian Ministries, 1991.

Handford, Elizabeth Rice. *Women Under the Judges.* Chattanooga: Joyful Christian Ministries, 1993.

Handford, Elizabeth Rice. *Women Under the Kings.* Chattanooga: Joyful Christian Ministries, 1995.

Harrison, Everett F. and Charles F. Pfeiffer., ed. *Wycliffe Commentary.* Chicago: The Moody Bible Institute, 1962.

Sources (continued)

Henry, Matthew. *Matthew Henry's Commentary, Vol. II, V, and VI.* Fleming H. Revell Company.

Horton, Robert F. *Women of the Old Testament.* London: Service and Paton, 1899.

Jensen, Mary E. *Bible Women Speak to Us Today.* Minneapolis: Augsburg Publishing House, 1983.

Jones, Beneth Peters. *Lights on Main Street.* Greenville: Bob Jones University Press, 2002.

Jones, Beneth Peters. *The Wilderness Within.* Greenville: Bob Jones University Press, 2002.

Karssen, Gien. *Her Name is Woman, Books 1 & 2.* Colorado Springs: Navpress, 1991.

Kempis, Thomas A. *The Imitation of Christ – Book 1.* Macon, Georgia: Mercer University Press, 1989.

Kuyper, Abraham. *Women of the New Testament.* Grand Rapids: Zondervan Publishing House, 1934 (renewed 1962).

Lockyer, Herbert. *All the Women of the Bible.* Grand Rapids: Zondervan Publishing House.

Matheson, George. *Portraits of Bible Women.* Grand Rapids: Kregel Publications, 1986.

McAllister, Grace. *God Portrays Women.* Chicago: Moody Press, 1954.

McGee, J. Vernon. *Through the Bible With J. Vernon McGee Vol. 2 and 4.* Nashville: Thomas Nelson, Inc., 1981.

Sources (continued)

Morton, H.V. *Women of the Bible.* New York: Dodd, Mead, and Company, 1941.

Nave, Orville J. *Nave's Topical Bible.* McLean, Virginia: MacDonald Publishing Company.

Orr, James. *The International Standard Bible Encyclopedia.* Grand Rapids: Wm. B. Erdman's Publishing Co., 1939, 1956.

Poole, Matthew. *A Commentary on the Holy Bible, Vol. I.* McLean, Virginia: MacDonald Publishing Company.

Price, Eugenia. *God Speaks to Women Today.* Grand Rapids: Zondervan Publishing House, 1964.

Purcell, Juanita. *Be Still, My Child.* Schaumburg, Illinois: Regular Baptist Press, 1997.

Ryrie, Charles Caldwell. *The Ryrie Study Bible.* Chicago: Moody Press, 1978.

Spurgeon, Charles H. *Spurgeon's Sermons on New Testament Women (Book One).* Grand Rapids: Kregel Publications, 1994.

Spurgeon, Charles H. *The Treasury of the Bible, Vol. I.* Grand Rapids: Baker Book House, 1988.

Tenney, Merrill, C. (Gen. ed.) *Pictorial Bible Dictionary,* Nashville: The Southwestern Company, 1974.

Unger, Merrill F. *The New Unger's Bible Dictionary.* Chicago: Moody Press, 1988.

Sources (continued)

Vine, W.E., Unger, Merrill, F., and William White, Jr. *Vine's Expository Dictionary of Biblical Words.* Nashville, Camden, New York: Thomas Nelson Publishers, 1985.

Voss, Carroll. *Women of the Old Testament.* Philadelphia: Women's Missionary Society of the United Lutheran Church in America, 1954.

Webster's Dictionary. Miami: P.S. I. Associates, 1986 ed.

Wiersbe, Warren. *Through The Year.* Grand Rapids: Baker Books, 1999.

Zodhiates, Spiros, Th.D. *The Complete Word Study New Testament.* Chattanooga: AMG Publishers, 1991.